P9-DLZ-830

PRESENTED TO:

Dani
_____

FROM:

Kanyo
_____

DATE:

1-18-2019
_____

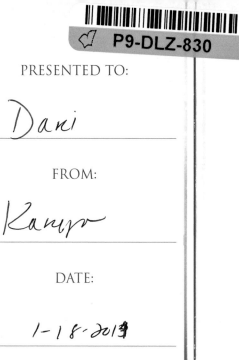

RELEASE!

letting
go of
life's
challenges
one worry at a time.

The quoted ideas expressed in this book (but not Scripture verses) are not, in all cases, exact quotations, as some have been edited for clarity and brevity. In all cases, the author has attempted to maintain the speaker's original intent. In some cases, quoted material for this book was obtained from secondary sources, primarily print media. While every effort was made to ensure the accuracy of these sources, the accuracy cannot be guaranteed. For additions, deletions, corrections, or clarifications in future editions of this text, please write Freeman-Smith.

Scripture quotations are taken from:

The Holy Bible, King James Version (KJV)

The Holy Bible, New International Version (NIV) Copyright © 1973, 1978, 1984, by International Bible Society. Used by permission of Zondervan Publishing House. All rights reserved.

The Holy Bible, New King James Version (NKJV) Copyright © 1982 by Thomas Nelson, Inc. Used by permission.

Holy Bible, New Living Translation, (NLT) copyright © 1996. Used by permission of Tyndale House Publishers, Inc., Wheaton, Illinois 60189. All rights reserved.

The Message (MSG)- This edition issued by contractual arrangement with NavPress, a division of The Navigators, U.S.A. Originally published by NavPress in English as THE MESSAGE: The Bible in Contemporary Language copyright 2002-2003 by Eugene Peterson. All rights reserved.

New Century Version®. (NCV) Copyright © 1987, 1988, 1991 by Word Publishing, a division of Thomas Nelson, Inc. All rights reserved. Used by permission.

The New American Standard Bible®, (NASB) Copyright © 1960, 1962, 1963, 1968, 1971, 1972, 1973, 1975, 1977, 1995 by The Lockman Foundation. Used by permission.

The Holy Bible, The Living Bible (TLB), Copyright © 1971 owned by assignment by Illinois Regional Bank N.A. (as trustee). Used by permission of Tyndale House Publishers, Inc., Wheaton, Illinois 60189. All rights reserved.

The Holman Christian Standard Bible™ (HCSB) Copyright © 1999, 2000, 2001 by Holman Bible Publishers. Used by permission.

Cover Design by Kim Russell / Wahoo Designs
Page Layout by Bart Dawson

ISBN 978-1-60587-346-6

Printed in the United States of America

INTRODUCTION

L ife would be so much easier (easier, but not better) if your faith were never challenged—if you never experienced doubts, or temptations, or worries, or frustrations. But it doesn't work that way. Hundreds of times each day, your faith is challenged as God provides you with opportunities to do the right thing by overcoming a negative emotion, or by extending a helping hand, or by speaking an encouraging word, or by doing a thousand other seemingly insignificant tasks that make your world a kinder, gentler, happier place. When these opportunities occur, you have a choice: you can either accept God's challenge and follow His path, or you can ignore His calling and live with the consequences. The ideas in this book will encourage you to do the right thing by following God's lead and by putting your faith to work.

To God, there are no insignificant acts of kindness. For Him, there are no small favors, no unimportant good deeds, no minor acts of mercy, and no inconsequential acts of obedience. To God, everything you do has major implications within His kingdom. He takes your actions seriously, and so should you.

This book contains devotional readings that are intended to help you address your concerns one worry at a time. The text is divided into 30 chapters, one for each day of the month. Each chapter contains Bible verses, quotations, brief essays, and timely tips, all of which can help you focus your thoughts on the countless blessings and opportunities that God has placed before you.

During the next 30 days, please try this experiment: read one chapter each morning. If you're already committed to a daily worship time, this book will enrich that experience. If you are not, the simple act of giving God a few minutes each morning will change the tone and direction of your life.

Your daily devotional time can be habit-forming, and should be. The first few minutes of each day are invaluable. So treat them that way, and offer them to God.

DAY 1

WHERE TO TAKE
YOUR WORRIES

Don't worry about anything, but in everything,
through prayer and petition with thanksgiving,
let your requests be made known to God.

—

PHILIPPIANS 4:6 HCSB

Never yield to gloomy anticipation.
Place your hope and confidence in God.
He has no record of failure.

—

MRS. CHARLES E. COWMAN

Because we have the ability to think, we also have the ability to worry. All of us, even the most faithful believers, are plagued by occasional periods of discouragement and doubt. Even though we hold tightly to God's promise of salvation—even though we sincerely believe in God's love and protection—we may find ourselves fretting over the countless details of everyday life.

Because of His humanity, Jesus understood the inevitability of worry. And He addressed the topic clearly and forcefully in the sixth chapter of Matthew:

Therefore I say to you, do not worry about your life, what you will eat or what you will drink; nor about your body, what you will put on. Is not life more than food and the body more than clothing? Look at the birds of the air, for they neither sow nor reap nor gather into barns; yet your heavenly Father feeds them. Are you not of more value than they? Which of you by worrying can add one cubit to his stature? . . . Therefore do not worry about tomorrow, for tomorrow will worry about its own things. Sufficient for the day is its own trouble. (vv. 25-27, 34 NKJV)

More often than not, our worries stem from an inability to focus and to trust. We fail to focus on a priceless gift from God: the profound, precious, present moment. Instead of thanking God for the blessings of this day, we choose to fret about two more ominous days: yesterday and tomorrow. We stew about the unfairness of the past, or we agonize about the uncertainty of the future. Such thinking stirs up negative feelings that prepare our hearts and minds for an equally destructive emotion: fear.

Our fears are rooted in a failure to trust. Instead of trusting God's plans for our lives, we fix our minds on countless troubles that might come to pass (but seldom do). A better strategy, of course, is to take God at His word by trusting His promises. Our Lord has promised that He will care for our needs—needs, by the way, that He understands far more completely than we do. God's Word is unambiguous; so, too, should be our trust in Him.

In Matthew 6, Jesus instructs us to live in day-tight compartments. He reminds us that each day has enough worries of its own without the added weight of yesterday's regrets or tomorrow's fears. Perhaps you feel disturbed by the past or threatened by the future. Perhaps you are concerned about your relationships, your health, or your finances. Or perhaps you are simply a "worrier" by nature. If so, make Matthew 6 a regular part of your daily Bible reading. This beautiful passage will remind you that God still sits in His heaven and you are His beloved child.

Then, perhaps, you will worry less and trust God more. And that's as it should be because God is trustworthy... and you are protected.

Worries carry responsibilities that belong to God, not to you. Worry does not enable us to escape evil; it makes us unfit to cope with it when it comes.

—

CORRIE TEN BOOM

MORE FROM GOD'S WORD ABOUT
OVERCOMING ANXIETY

I will be with you when you pass through the waters . . . when you walk through the fire . . . the flame will not burn you. For I the Lord your God, the Holy One of Israel, and your Savior.

ISAIAH 43:2-3 HCSB

Your heart must not be troubled. Believe in God; believe also in Me.

JOHN 14:1 HCSB

Come to Me, all you who labor and are heavy laden, and I will give you rest. Take My yoke upon you and learn from Me, for I am gentle and lowly in heart, and you will find rest for your souls. For My yoke is easy and My burden is light.

MATTHEW 11:28-30 NKJV

Be strong and courageous, and do the work. Don't be afraid or discouraged, for the Lord God, my God, is with you. He won't leave you or forsake you.

1 CHRONICLES 28:20 HCSB

MORE POWERFUL IDEAS ABOUT WORRY

Worry is the senseless process of cluttering up tomorrow's opportunities with leftover problems from today.

BARBARA JOHNSON

Pray, and let God worry.

MARTIN LUTHER

Today is mine. Tomorrow is none of my business. If I peer anxiously into the fog of the future, I will strain my spiritual eyes so that I will not see clearly what is required of me now.

ELISABETH ELLIOTT

A TIP FOR TODAY

You have worries, but God has solutions. Your challenge is to trust Him to solve the problems that you can't.

Worry and anxiety are sand in the machinery of life; faith is the oil.

E. STANLEY JONES

Anxiety may be natural and normal for the world, but it is not to be part of a believer's lifestyle.

KAY ARTHUR

14

A PRAYER FOR TODAY

Lord, sometimes this world is a difficult place, and, as a frail human being, I am fearful. When I am worried, restore my faith. When I am anxious, turn my thoughts to You. When I grieve, touch my heart with Your enduring love. Give me the wisdom to trust in You, Father, and give me the courage to live a life of faith, not a life of fear. Amen

TODAY'S THOUGHTS

My thoughts about the need to trust God and to embrace the changes that He has placed along my path.

_____

_____

_____

_____

_____

_____

_____

_____

_____

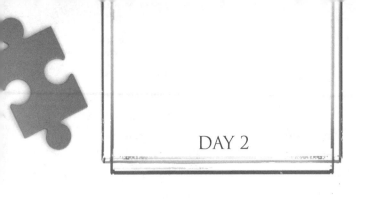

DAY 2

EMBRACING CHANGE

His message was simple and austere,
like his desert surroundings:
"Change your life. God's kingdom is here."

—

MATTHEW 3:2 MSG

Resistance to change is universal.
It invades all classes and cultures.
There is nothing more difficult to undertake or
more uncertain in its success,
than introducing change.

JOHN MAXWELL

I n our fast-paced world, everyday life has become an exercise in managing change. Our circumstances change; our relationships change; our bodies change. We grow older every day, as does our world. Thankfully, God does not change. He is eternal, as are the truths that are found in His Holy Word.

The ideas in this book are intended to help you accept change—and embrace it—as you continue to seek God's unfolding plan for your life.

Are you facing one of life's inevitable "mid-course corrections"? If so, you must place your faith, your trust, and your life in the hands of the One who does not change: your Heavenly Father. He is the unmoving rock upon which you must construct this day and every day. When you do, you are secure.

ANTICIPATING YOUR
NEXT GRAND ADVENTURE

It has been said that a rut is nothing more than a grave with both ends kicked out. That's a thought worth pondering. Have you made your life an exciting adventure, or have you allowed the distractions of everyday life to rob you of a sense of God's purpose?

As a believing Christian, you have every reason to celebrate. So if you find yourself feeling as if you're stuck in a rut, or in an unfortunate circumstance, or in a difficult relationship, abandon the status quo by making the changes that your heart tells you are right. After all, in God's glorious kingdom, there should be no place for disciples who are dejected, discouraged, or disheartened. God has a far better plan than that, and so should you.

> With God, it isn't who you were that matters;
> it's who you are becoming.
>
> —
>
> LIZ CURTIS HIGGS

MORE FROM GOD'S WORD ABOUT TRUST

Trust in the Lord with all your heart, and do not rely on your own understanding; think about Him in all your ways, and He will guide you on the right paths.

PROVERBS 3:5-6 HCSB

Let us hold fast the confession of our hope without wavering, for He who promised is faithful.

HEBREWS 10:23 NKJV

For we walk by faith, not by sight.

2 CORINTHIANS 5:7 NKJV

The one who understands a matter finds success, and the one who trusts in the Lord will be happy.

PROVERBS 16:20 HCSB

For the eyes of the Lord range throughout the earth to show Himself strong for those whose hearts are completely His.

2 CHRONICLES 16:9 HCSB

MORE POWERFUL IDEAS ABOUT CHANGE

More often than not, when something looks like it's the absolute end, it is really the beginning.

CHARLES SWINDOLL

In a world kept chaotic by change, you will eventually discover, as I have, that this is one of the most precious qualities of the God we are looking for: He doesn't change.

BILL HYBELS

Mere change is not growth. Growth is the synthesis of change and continuity, and where there is no continuity there is no growth.

C. S. LEWIS

A TIP FOR TODAY

Change is inevitable. Don't fear it. Embrace it.

The secret of contentment in the midst of change is found in having roots in the changeless Christ—the same yesterday, today and forever.

ED YOUNG

A PRAYER FOR TODAY

Dear Lord, our world is constantly changing. When I face the inevitable transitions of life, I will turn to You for strength and assurance. Thank You, Father, for love that is unchanging and everlasting. Amen

TODAY'S THOUGHTS

My thoughts about the need to embrace the changes that God has placed along my path.

_____

_____

_____

_____

_____

_____

_____

_____

_____

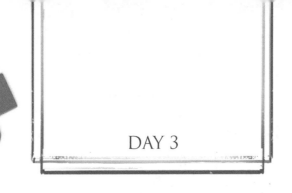

DAY 3

GOD DOES NOT CHANGE

Be still, and know that I am God.

—

PSALM 46:10 NKJV

Number one, God brought me here. It is by His will that
I am in this place. In that fact I will rest.
Number two, He will keep me here in His love and
give me grace to behave as His child.
Number three, He will make the trial a blessing,
teaching me the lessons He intends for me to learn and
working in me the grace He means to bestow.
Number four, in His good time He can
bring me out again. How and when, He knows.
So, let me say I am here.

—

ANDREW MURRAY

These are times of great uncertainty. As we become accustomed to, and at times almost numbed by, a steady stream of unsettling news, we are reminded that our world is in a state of constant change. But God is not. So when the world seems to be trembling beneath our feet, we can be comforted in the knowledge that our Heavenly Father is the rock that cannot be shaken. His Word promises, "I am the Lord, I do not change" (Malachi 3:6 NKJV).

Every day that we live, we mortals encounter a multitude of changes—some good, some not so good. And on occasion, all of us must endure life-changing personal losses that leave us heartbroken. When we do, our Heavenly

Father stands ready to comfort us, to guide us, and—in time—to heal us.

Is the world spinning a little too fast for your liking? Are you facing troubling uncertainties, difficult circumstances, or unwelcome changes? If so, please remember that God is far bigger than any problem you may face. So, instead of worrying about life's inevitable challenges, put your faith in the Father and His only begotten Son. After all, "Jesus Christ is the same yesterday, today, and forever" (Hebrews 13:8 NKJV). And it is precisely because your Savior does not change that you can face your challenges with courage for today and hope for tomorrow.

Are you anxious about situations that you cannot control? Take your anxieties to God. Are you troubled? Take your troubles to Him. Does your little corner of the universe seem to be a frightening place? Seek protection from the One who cannot be moved. The same God who created the universe will protect you if you ask Him . . . so ask Him . . . and then serve Him with willing hands and a trusting heart.

MORE FROM GOD'S WORD ABOUT HIS LOVE

We know how much God loves us, and we have put our trust in him. God is love, and all who live in love live in God, and God lives in them.

1 JOHN 4:16 NLT

As the Father loved Me, I also have loved you; abide in My love.

JOHN 15:9 NKJV

The unfailing love of the LORD never ends! By his mercies we have been kept from complete destruction.

LAMENTATIONS 3:22 NLT

Whoever is wise will observe these things, and they will understand the lovingkindness of the Lord.

PSALM 107:43 NKJV

For God loved the world in this way: He gave His only Son, so that everyone who believes in Him will not perish but have eternal life.

JOHN 3:16 HCSB

MORE POWERFUL IDEAS ABOUT
GOD'S PROTECTION

Sometimes we need a birds-eye view of what God sees about our lives. If we could just see what he sees we might lighten up a little bit.

DENNIS SWANBERG

Under heaven's lock and key, we are protected by the most efficient security system available: the power of God.

CHARLES SWINDOLL

There is not only fear, but terrible danger, for the life unguarded by God.

OSWALD CHAMBERS

A TIP FOR TODAY

God is here, and He wants to establish an intimate relationship with you. When you sincerely reach out to Him, you will sense His presence.

He is within and without. His Spirit dwells within me. His armor protects me. He goes before me and is behind me.

MARY MORRISON SUGGS

A PRAYER FOR TODAY

Dear Lord, Your love is eternal and Your laws are everlasting. When I obey Your commandments, I am blessed. Today, I invite You to reign over every corner of my heart. I will have faith in You, Father. I will sense Your presence; I will accept Your love; I will trust Your will; and I will praise You for the Savior of my life: Your Son, Jesus. Amen

TODAY'S THOUGHTS

My thoughts about God's power and His love.

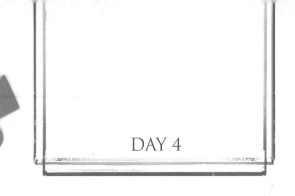

DAY 4

ACCEPTING ADVICE

A wise man will hear and increase learning,
and a man of understanding
will attain wise counsel.

PROVERBS 1:5 NKJV

God guides through the counsel of good people.

E. STANLEY JONES

If you find yourself caught up in a difficult situation, it's time to start searching for knowledgeable friends and mentors who can give you solid advice. Why do you need help evaluating the person in the mirror? Because you're simply too close to that person, that's why. Sometimes, you'll be tempted to give yourself straight As when you deserve considerably lower grades. On other occasions, you'll become your own worst critic, giving yourself a string of failing marks when you deserve better. The truth, of course, is often somewhere in the middle.

Finding a wise mentor is only half the battle. It takes just as much wisdom—and sometimes more—to act upon good advice as it does to give it. So find people you can trust, listen to them carefully, and act accordingly.

FIND A MENTOR

If you're going through tough times, it's helpful to find mentors who have been there and done that—people who have experienced your particular challenge and lived to tell about it.

When you find mentors who are godly men and women, you become a more godly person yourself. That's why you should seek out advisors who, by their words and their presence, make you a better person and a better Christian.

Today, as a gift to yourself, select, from your friends and family members, a mentor whose judgment you trust. Then listen carefully to your mentor's advice and be willing to accept that advice, even if accepting it requires effort, or pain, or both. Consider your mentor to be God's gift to you. Thank God for that gift, and use it for the glory of His kingdom.

MORE FROM GOD'S WORD ABOUT
ACCEPTING ADVICE

He is God. Let him do whatever he thinks best.

1 SAMUEL 3:18 MSG

It is better to be a poor but wise youth than to be an old and foolish king who refuses all advice.

ECCLESIASTES 4:13 NLT

It is better to listen to rebuke from a wise person than to listen to the song of fools.

ECCLESIASTES 7:5 HCSB

Know-it-alls don't like being told what to do; they avoid the company of wise men and women.

PROVERBS 15:12 MSG

Listen to counsel and receive instruction so that you may be wise in later life.

PROVERBS 19:20 HCSB

MORE POWERFUL IDEAS ABOUT MENTORS

A single word, if spoken in a friendly spirit, may be sufficient to turn one from dangerous error.

FANNY CROSBY

No matter how crazy or nutty your life has seemed, God can make something strong and good out of it. He can help you grow wide branches for others to use as shelter.

BARBARA JOHNSON

God often keeps us on the path by guiding us through the counsel of friends and trusted spiritual advisors.

BILL HYBELS

A TIP FOR TODAY

If you can't seem to listen to constructive criticism with an open mind, ask God to soften your heart, open your ears, and enlighten your mind.

Yes, the Spirit was sent to be our Counselor. Yes, Jesus speaks to us personally. But often he works through another human being.

JOHN ELDREDGE

A PRAYER FOR TODAY

Dear Lord, thank You for the mentors whom You have placed along my path. When I am troubled, let me turn to them for help, for guidance, for comfort, and for perspective. And Father, let me be a friend and mentor to others, so that my love for You may be demonstrated by my genuine concern for them. Amen

TODAY'S THOUGHTS

My thoughts about the importance of finding—and listening to—trustworthy mentors.

_____

_____

_____

_____

_____

_____

_____

_____

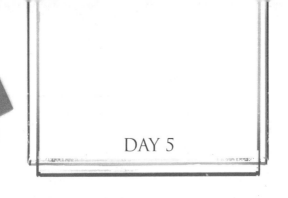

DAY 5

GOD'S PLAN AND YOUR TOUGH TIMES

Who are those who fear the Lord?
He will show them the path they should choose.
They will live in prosperity, and their children
will inherit the Promised Land.

—

PSALM 25:12-13 NLT

Every misfortune, every failure,
every loss may be transformed.
God has the power to transform all misfortunes
into "God-sends."

—

MRS. CHARLES E. COWMAN

I t's an age-old riddle: Why does God allow us to endure tough times? After all, since we trust that God is
all-powerful, and since we trust that His hand shapes
our lives, why doesn't He simply rescue us—and our loved
ones—from all hardship and pain?

God's Word teaches us again and again that He loves
us and wants the best for us. And the Bible also teaches us
that God is ever-present and always watchful. So why, we
wonder, if God is really so concerned with every detail of
our lives, does He permit us to endure emotions like grief,
sadness, shame, or fear? And why does He allow tragic
circumstances to invade the lives of good people? These
questions perplex us, especially when times are tough.

On occasion, all of us face adversity, and throughout
life, we all must endure life-changing personal losses that
leave us breathless. When we pass through the dark valleys of life, we often ask, "Why me?" Sometimes, of course,
the answer is obvious—sometimes we make mistakes, and
we must pay for them. But on other occasions, when we

have done nothing wrong, we wonder why God allows us to suffer.

Even when we cannot understand God's plans, we must trust them. And even when we are impatient for our situations to improve, we must trust God's timing. If we seek to live in accordance with His plan for our lives, we must continue to study His Word (in good times and bad), and we must be watchful for His signs, knowing that in time, He will lead us through the valleys, onward to the mountaintop.

So if you're enduring tough times, don't give up and don't give in. God still has glorious plans for you. So keep your eyes and ears open . . . as well as your heart.

FINDING NEW MEANING

Perhaps tough times have turned your world upside down. Maybe it seems to you as if everything in your life has been rearranged. Or perhaps your relationships and your responsibilities have been permanently altered. If so, you may come face to face with the daunting task of finding new purpose for your life. And God is willing to help.

God has an important plan for your life, and part of His plan may well be related to the tough times you're experiencing. After all, you've learned important, albeit hard-earned, lessons. And you're certainly wiser today than you were yesterday. So your suffering carries with it great potential: the potential for intense personal growth and the potential to help others.

As you begin to reorganize your life, look for ways to use your experiences for the betterment of others. When you do, you can rest assured that the course of your recovery will depend upon how quickly you discover new people to help and new reasons to live. And as you move through and beyond your own particular tough times, be mindful of this fact: as a survivor, you will have countless opportunities to serve others. By serving others, you will bring glory to God and meaning to the hardships you've endured.

Don't let circumstances distress you. Rather, look for the will of God for your life to be revealed in and through those circumstances.

BILLY GRAHAM

MORE FROM GOD'S WORD ABOUT HIS PLAN

"For I know the plans I have for you," declares the Lord, "plans to prosper you and not to harm you, plans to give you hope and a future. Then you will call upon me and come and pray to me, and I will listen to you."

JEREMIAH 29:11-12 NIV

And we know that in all things God works for the good of those who love him, who have been called according to his purpose.

ROMANS 8:28 NIV

He replied, "Every plant that My heavenly Father didn't plant will be uprooted."

MATTHEW 15:13 HCSB

The steps of the Godly are directed by the Lord. He delights in every detail of their lives. Though they stumble, they will not fall, for the Lord holds them by the hand.

PSALM 37:23-24 NLT

It is God who works in you to will and to act according to his good purpose.

PHILIPPIANS 2:13 NIV

MORE POWERFUL IDEAS ABOUT GOD'S PLAN

Each problem is a God-appointed instructor.

CHARLES SWINDOLL

When terrible things happen, there are two choices, and only two: We can trust God, or we can defy Him. We believe that God is God, He's still got the whole world in His hands and knows exactly what He's doing, or we must believe that He is not God and that we are at the awful mercy of mere chance.

ELISABETH ELLIOT

This battle is not yours—it's the Lord's!

ANONYMOUS

Our loving God uses difficulty in our lives to burn away the sin of self and build faith and spiritual power.

BILL BRIGHT

A TIP FOR TODAY

Waiting faithfully for God's plan to unfold is more important than understanding it. So when you can't understand God's plans, trust Him and never lose faith!

A PRAYER FOR TODAY

Dear Lord, even when I am discouraged, even when my heart is heavy, I will earnestly seek Your will for my life. You have a plan for me that I can never fully understand. But You understand. And I will trust You today, tomorrow, and forever. Amen

TODAY'S THOUGHTS

My thoughts about the importance of cultivating the plan God has for my life.

_____

_____

_____

_____

_____

_____

_____

_____

_____

_____

DAY 6

MANAGING STRESS

*The peace of God, which surpasses
all understanding, will guard your hearts and
minds through Christ Jesus.*

—

PHILIPPIANS 4:7 NKJV

Stress is the intangible partner of progress.

—

CHARLES STANLEY

Stressful days are an inevitable fact of modern life. And how do we best cope with the challenges of our demanding world? By turning our days and our lives over to God. Elisabeth Elliot writes, "If my life is surrendered to God, all is well. Let me not grab it back, as though it were in peril in His hand but would be safer in mine!" Yet even the most devout Christian may, at times, seek to grab the reins of her life and proclaim, "I'm in charge!" To do so is foolish, prideful, and stressful.

When we seek to impose our own wills upon the world—or upon other people—we invite stress into our lives . . . needlessly. But, when we turn our lives and our hearts over to God—when we accept His will instead of seeking vainly to impose our own—we discover the inner peace that can be ours through Him.

Do you feel overwhelmed by the stresses of daily life? Turn your concerns and your prayers over to God. Trust Him completely. When it comes to the inevitable challenges of this day, hand them over to God completely and without reservation. He knows your needs and will meet those needs in His own way and in His own time if you let Him.

SLOWING DOWN THE MERRY-GO-ROUND

Every major change, whether bad or good, puts stress on you and your family. That's why it's sensible to plan things so that you don't invite too many changes into your life at once. Of course: you'll be tempted to do otherwise. Once you land that new job, you'll be sorely tempted to buy the new house and the new car. Or if you've just gotten married, you'll be tempted to buy everything in sight—while the credit card payments mount. Don't do it!

When it comes to making big changes or big purchases, proceed slowly. Otherwise, you may find yourself uncomfortably perched atop a merry-go-round that is much easier to start than it is to stop.

God, who comforts the downcast, comforted us . . . .

—

2 CORINTHIANS 7:6 NIV

43

MORE FROM GOD'S WORD ABOUT
OVERCOMING ADVERSITY

LORD, help! they cried in their trouble, and he saved them from their distress.

PSALM 107:13 NLT

You have allowed me to suffer much hardship, but you will restore me to life again and lift me up from the depths of the earth. You will restore me to even greater honor and comfort me once again.

PSALM 71:20-21 NLT

When my heart is overwhelmed: lead me to the rock that is higher than I.

PSALM 61:2 KJV

Trust God from the bottom of your heart; don't try to figure out everything on your own. Listen for God's voice in everything you do, everywhere you go; he's the one who will keep you on track.

PROVERBS 3:5-6 MSG

MORE POWERFUL IDEAS ABOUT MANAGING STRESS

The happiest people I know are the ones who have learned how to hold everything loosely and have given the worrisome, stress-filled, fearful details of their lives into God's keeping.

CHARLES SWINDOLL

When frustrations develop into problems that stress you out, the best way to cope is to stop, catch your breath, and do something for yourself, not out of selfishness, but out of wisdom.

BARBARA JOHNSON

The better acquainted you become with God, the less tensions you feel and the more peace you possess.

CHARLES ALLEN

Don't be overwhelmed. Take it one day and one prayer at a time.

STORMIE OMARTIAN

A TIP FOR TODAY

If you're experiencing too much stress, you should make sure that you're not neglecting your prayer life.

45

A PRAYER FOR TODAY

Dear Lord, sometimes the stresses of the day leave me tired and frustrated. Renew my energy, Father, and give me perspective and peace. Let me draw comfort and courage from Your promises, from Your love, and from Your Son. Amen

TODAY'S THOUGHTS

My thoughts about some common-sense ways that I can manage stress.

_____

_____

_____

_____

_____

_____

_____

_____

_____

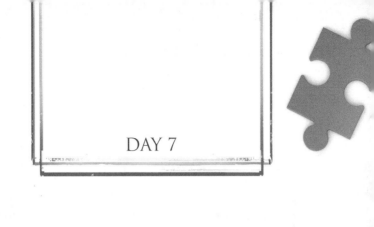

DAY 7

UNDERSTANDING
DEPRESSION

Weeping may go on all night,
but joy comes with the morning.

—

PSALM 30:5 NLT

There is no pit so deep
that God's love is not deeper still.

—

CORRIE TEN BOOM

Throughout our lives, all of us must endure personal losses that leave us struggling to find hope. The sadness that accompanies such losses is an inescapable fact of life—but in time, we move beyond our grief as the sadness runs its course and life returns to normal. Depression, however, is more than sadness . . . much more.

Depression is a physical and emotional condition that is, in almost all cases, treatable with medication and counseling. And it is not a disease to be taken lightly. Left untreated, depression presents real dangers to patients' physical health and to their emotional well-being.

If you're feeling blue, perhaps it's a logical response to the disappointments of everyday life. But if your feelings of sadness have lasted longer than you think they should—or if someone close to you fears that your sadness may have evolved into clinical depression—it's time to seek professional help.

Here are a few simple guidelines to consider as you make decisions about possible medical treatment:

1. If your feelings of sadness have resulted in persistent and prolonged changes in sleep patterns, or if you've

experienced a significant change in weight (either gain or loss), consult your physician. 2. If you have persistent urges toward self-destructive behavior, or if you feel as though you have lost the will to live, consult a professional counselor or physician immediately. 3. If someone you trust urges you to seek counseling, schedule a session with a professionally trained counselor to evaluate your condition. 4. If you are plagued by consistent, prolonged, severe feelings of hopelessness, consult a physician, a professional counselor, or your pastor.

God's Word has much to say about every aspect of your life, including your emotional health. And, when you face concerns of any sort—including symptoms of depression—remember that God is with you. Your Creator intends that His joy should become your joy. Yet sometimes, amid the inevitable hustle and bustle of life, you may forfeit—albeit temporarily—God's joy as you wrestle with the challenges of daily living.

So, if you're feeling genuinely depressed, trust your medical doctor to do his or her part. Then, place your ultimate trust in your benevolent Heavenly Father. His healing touch, like His love, endures forever.

MORE FROM GOD'S WORD ABOUT HIS SUPPORT

Now the God of all grace, who called you to His eternal glory in Christ Jesus, will personally restore, establish, strengthen, and support you.

1 PETER 5:10 HCSB

The LORD is my strength and song, and He has become my salvation; He is my God, and I will praise Him . . .

EXODUS 15:2 NKJV

Peace, peace to you, and peace to your helpers! For your God helps you.

1 CHRONICLES 12:18 NKJV

He gives power to the weak, and to those who have no might He increases strength.

ISAIAH 40:29 NKJV

I am able to do all things through Him who strengthens me.

PHILIPPIANS 4:13 HCSB

MORE POWERFUL IDEAS ABOUT NEGATIVE EMOTIONS

Emotions we have not poured out in the safe hands of God can turn into feelings of hopelessness and depression. God is safe.

BETH MOORE

God is a specialist; He is well able to work our failures into His plans. Often the doorway to success is entered through the hallway of failure.

ERWIN LUTZER

Feelings of uselessness and hopelessness are not from God, but from the evil one, the devil, who wants to discourage you and thwart your effectiveness for the Lord.

BILL BRIGHT

I am sure it is never sadness—a proper, straight, natural response to loss—that does people harm, but all the other things, all the resentment, dismay, doubt and self-pity with which it is usually complicated.

C. S. LEWIS

A TIP FOR TODAY

Depression is serious business, and it's a highly treatable disease . . . treat it that way.

A PRAYER FOR TODAY

Dear Lord, You have promised to place a new song on my lips. If the darkness envelops me, Father, remind me of those promises. And, give me the wisdom to accept help from the people You have placed along my path. Amen

TODAY'S THOUGHTS

My thoughts about God's promise to love me and protect me today and forever.

_____

_____

_____

_____

_____

_____

_____

_____

_____

_____

DAY 8

BEYOND FEAR

Indeed, God is my salvation.
I will trust [Him] and not be afraid.

—

ISAIAH 12:2 HCSB

Fear is a self-imposed prison that will keep you from
becoming what God intends for you to be.

—

RICK WARREN

All of us may find our courage tested by the inevitable disappointments and tragedies of life. After all, ours is a world filled with uncertainty, hardship, sickness, and danger. Old Man Trouble, it seems, is never too far from the front door.

When we focus upon our fears and our doubts, we may find many reasons to lie awake at night and fret about the uncertainties of the coming day. A better strategy, of course, is to focus not upon our fears, but instead upon our God.

God is as near as your next breath, and He is in control. He offers salvation to all His children, including you. God is your shield and your strength; you are His forever. So don't focus your thoughts upon the fears of the day. Instead, trust God's plan and His eternal love for you. And remember: God is good, and He has the last word.

GOD CAN HANDLE IT

It's a promise that is made over and over again in the Bible: whatever "it" is, God can handle it.

Life isn't always easy. Far from it! Sometimes, life can be very, very tough. But even then, even during our darkest moments, we're protected by a loving Heavenly Father. When we're worried, God can reassure us; when we're sad, God can comfort us. When our hearts are broken, God is not just near; He is here. So we must lift our thoughts and prayers to Him. When we do, He will answer our prayers. Why? Because He is our Shepherd, and He has promised to protect us now and forever.

When we meditate on God and remember
the promises He has given us in His Word,
our faith grows, and our fears dissolve.

—

CHARLES STANLEY

55

MORE FROM GOD'S WORD ABOUT
OVERCOMING FEAR

Even when I go through the darkest valley, I fear [no] danger, for You are with me.

PSALM 23:4 HCSB

Don't be afraid. Only believe.

MARK 5:36 HCSB

For I, the Lord your God, hold your right hand and say to you: Do not fear, I will help you.

ISAIAH 41:13 HCSB

I sought the Lord, and He heard me, and delivered me from all my fears.

PSALM 34:4 NKJV

Do not fear, for I am with you; do not be afraid, for I am your God. I will strengthen you; I will help you; I will hold on to you with My righteous right hand.

ISAIAH 41:10 HCSB

MORE POWERFUL IDEAS ABOUT
OVERCOMING FEAR

God shields us from most of the things we fear, but when He chooses not to shield us, He unfailingly allots grace in the measure needed.

ELISABETH ELLIOT

Only believe, don't fear. Our Master, Jesus, always watches over us, and no matter what the persecution, Jesus will surely overcome it.

LOTTIE MOON

If we do not tremble before God, the world's system seems wonderful to us and pleasantly consumes us.

JAMES MONTGOMERY BOICE

The remarkable thing about fearing God is that when you fear God, you fear nothing else, whereas if you do not fear God, you fear everything else.

OSWALD CHAMBERS

A TIP FOR TODAY

If you're feeling fearful or anxious, you must trust God to solve the problems that are simply too big for you to solve.

A PRAYER FOR TODAY

Dear Lord, let Your purposes be my purposes. Let Your priorities be my priorities. Let Your will be my will. Let Your Word be my guide. And, let me grow in faith and in wisdom today and every day. Amen

TODAY'S THOUGHTS

My thoughts about the need to prayerfully ask God to direct my steps and guide my plans.

_____

_____

_____

_____

_____

_____

_____

_____

_____

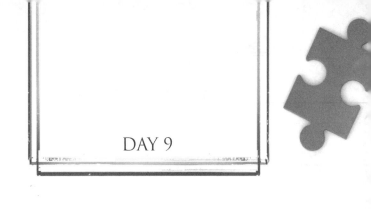

DAY 9

OVERCOMING ADVERSITY

*We also have joy with our troubles, because we
know that these troubles produce patience.
And patience produces character,
and character produces hope.*

—

ROMANS 5:3-4 NCV

Through all of the crises of life—
and we all are going to experience them—
we have this magnificent Anchor.

—

FRANKLIN GRAHAM

As life here on earth unfolds, all of us encounter occasional disappointments and setbacks: those occasional visits from Old Man Trouble are simply a fact of life, and none of us are exempt. When tough times arrive, we may be forced to rearrange our plans and our priorities. But even on our darkest days, we must remember that God's love remains constant.

The fact that we encounter adversity is not nearly so important as the way we choose to deal with it. When tough times arrive, we have a clear choice: we can begin the difficult work of tackling our troubles . . . or not. When we summon the courage to look Old Man Trouble squarely in the eye, he usually blinks. But, if we refuse to address our problems, even the smallest annoyances have a way of growing into king-sized catastrophes.

As believers, we know that God loves us and that He will protect us. In times of hardship, He will comfort us; in times of sorrow, He will dry our tears. When we are troubled, or weak, or sorrowful, God is always with us. We must build our lives on the rock that cannot be shaken:

we must trust in God. And then, we must get on with the hard work of tackling our problems . . . because if we don't, who will? Or should?

WHEN YOUR FAITH IS TESTED

Life is a tapestry of good days and difficult days, with good days predominating. During the good days, we are tempted to take our blessings for granted (a temptation that we must resist with all our might). But, during life's difficult days, we discover precisely what we're made of. And more importantly, we discover what our faith is made of.

Has your faith been put to the test yet? If so, then you know that with God's help, you can endure life's darker days. But if you have not yet faced the inevitable trials and tragedies of life here on earth, don't worry: you will. And when your faith is put to the test, rest assured that God is perfectly willing—and always ready—to give you strength for the struggle.

MORE FROM GOD'S WORD ABOUT ADVERSITY

When you pass through the waters, I will be with you; and through the rivers, they shall not overflow you. When you walk through the fire, you shall not be burned, nor shall the flame scorch you. For I am the Lord your God, The Holy One of Israel, your Savior.

ISAIAH 43:2-3 NKJV

The LORD also will be a stronghold for the oppressed, a stronghold in times of trouble.

PSALM 9:9 NASB

You pulled me from the brink of death, my feet from the cliff-edge of doom. Now I stroll at leisure with God in the sunlit fields of life.

PSALM 56:13 MSG

Come to Me, all you who labor and are heavy laden, and I will give you rest. Take My yoke upon you and learn from Me, for I am gentle and lowly in heart, and you will find rest for your souls. For My yoke is easy and My burden is light.

MATTHEW 11:28-30 NKJV

MORE POWERFUL IDEAS ABOUT ADVERSITY

When problems threaten to engulf us, we must do what believers have always done, turn to the Lord for encouragement and solace. As Psalm 46:1 states, "God is our refuge and strength, an ever-present help in trouble."

SHIRLEY DOBSON

It's a good thing to have all the props pulled out from under us occasionally. It gives us some sense of what rock is under our feet, and what is sand. It stops us from taking anything for granted.

MADELEINE L'ENGLE

I believe that the Creator of this universe takes delight in turning the terrors and tragedies that come with living in this old, fallen domain of the devil and transforming them into something that strengthens our hope, tests our faith, and shows forth His glory.

AL GREEN

A TIP FOR TODAY

If you're having tough times, don't keep everything bottled up inside. Find a person you can really trust, and talk things over.

A PRAYER FOR TODAY

Dear Lord, when I face the inevitable disappointments of life, give me perspective and faith. When I am discouraged, give me the strength to trust Your promises and follow Your will. Then, when I have done my best, Father, let me live with the assurance that You are firmly in control, and that Your love endures forever. Amen

TODAY'S THOUGHTS

My thoughts about some of the lessons I've learned during tough times.

_____

_____

_____

_____

_____

_____

_____

_____

DAY 10

ENDURING THE LOSS
OF EMPLOYMENT

You are my hope; O Lord GOD,
You are my confidence.

—

PSALM 71:5 NASB

We can always get up and begin again.
Our God is the God of new beginnings.

—

WARREN WIERSBE

Whether we like it or not, we live in a highly competitive global economy. And whether we like it or not, our jobs, like the ever-changing world in which we live, are in a constant state of flux.

Losing one's job can be a traumatic experience. Job loss is usually a problem of the first magnitude, a problem that results in financial and emotional stress. But of this we can be certain: hidden beneath every problem is the seed of a solution—God's solution. Our challenge, as faithful believers, is to trust God's providence and seek His solutions. When we do, we eventually discover that God does nothing without a very good reason: His reason.

If you've recently experienced a job loss, here are some things to consider and some things to do:

1. Remember that God is still right here. He rules the mountaintops of life and the valleys, so don't lose hope. (Lamentations 3:25-26)

2. If you're feeling sorry for yourself, stop. Self-pity isn't going to help you find a better job or build a better life. (2 Timothy 1:7)

3. If you're out of a job, you have a critically important job: finding a new one. Don't delay; don't take an extended vacation; don't try to improve your golf game; don't watch daytime TV. If you need a new job, you should spend at least 40 hours a week looking for it. And you should keep doing so until you find the job you need. (1 Chronicles 28:20)

4. Use all available tools. Those tools include, but are not limited to, friends, family, church members, former business associates, classified advertisements, employment services, the Internet, and your own shoe leather. (2 Peter 1:5-6)

5. Think positive thoughts. Think positively about yourself, your abilities, and your future. After all, if you don't believe in those things, how can you expect your future employer to believe in them, either? (Philippians 4:8)

Jesus gives us the ultimate rest,
the confidence we need, to escape the frustration and
chaos of the world around us.

—

BILLY GRAHAM

MORE FROM GOD'S WORD ABOUT
NEW BEGINNINGS

Then the One seated on the throne said, "Look! I am making everything new."

REVELATION 21:5 HCSB

But those who wait on the Lord shall renew their strength; they shall mount up with wings like eagles, they shall run and not be weary, they shall walk and not faint.

ISAIAH 40:31 NKJV

Therefore if anyone is in Christ, he is a new creature; the old things passed away; behold, new things have come.

2 CORINTHIANS 5:17 HCSB

You are being renewed in the spirit of your minds; you put on the new man, the one created according to God's likeness in righteousness and purity of the truth.

EPHESIANS 4:23-24 HCSB

I will give you a new heart and put a new spirit within you.

EZEKIEL 36:26 HCSB

MORE POWERFUL IDEAS ABOUT CONFIDENCE

Bible hope is confidence in the future.

WARREN WIERSBE

If we indulge in any confidence that is not grounded on the Rock of Ages, our confidence is worse than a dream, it will fall on us and cover us with its ruins, causing sorrow and confusion.

C. H. SPURGEON

God's omniscience can instill you with a supernatural confidence that can transform your life.

BILL HYBELS

I'm convinced that there is nothing that can happen to me in this life that is not precisely designed by a sovereign Lord to give me the opportunity to learn to know Him.

ELISABETH ELLIOT

A TIP FOR TODAY

Keep looking until you find a job that is a good match for your particular skills. That job is out there . . . it's up to you to find it.

A PRAYER FOR TODAY

Dear Lord, make my work pleasing to You. Help me to sow the seeds of Your abundance everywhere I go. Let me be passionate in all my undertakings and give me patience to wait for Your harvest. Amen

TODAY'S THOUGHTS

My thoughts about the career that's best for me.

_____

_____

_____

_____

_____

_____

_____

_____

_____

_____

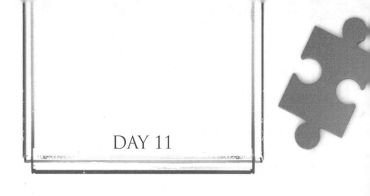

DAY 11

RENEWED DAY BY DAY

Every morning he wakes me.
He teaches me to listen like a student.
The Lord God helps me learn.

—

ISAIAH 50:4-5 NCV

The moment you wake up each morning,
all your wishes and hopes for the day rush at you
like wild animals. And the first job each morning
consists in shoving it all back; in listening to that
other voice, taking that other point of view,
letting that other, larger, stronger,
quieter life come flowing in.

—

C. S. LEWIS

Each new day is a gift from God, and if you are wise, you will spend a few quiet moments each morning thanking the Giver. When you do, you'll discover that time spent with God can lift your spirits and relieve your stress.

Warren Wiersbe writes, "Surrender your mind to the Lord at the beginning of each day." And that's sound advice. When you begin each day with your head bowed and your heart lifted, you are reminded of God's love, His protection, and His commandments. Then, you can align your priorities for the coming day with the teachings and commandments that God has placed upon your heart.

So, if you've acquired the unfortunate habit of trying to "squeeze" God into the corners of your life, it's time to reshuffle the items on your to-do list by placing God first. And if you haven't already done so, form the habit of spending quality time with your Father in heaven. He deserves it . . . and so do you.

PRAY ABOUT IT

Andrew Murray observed, "Some people pray just to pray, and some people pray to know God." Your task, as a maturing believer, is to pray, not out of habit or obligation, but out of a sincere desire to know your Heavenly Father. Through constant prayers, you should petition God, you should praise Him, and you seek to discover His unfolding plans for your life.

Today, reach out to the Giver of all blessings. Turn to Him for guidance and for strength. Invite Him into every corner of your day. Ask Him to teach you and to lead you. And remember that no matter your circumstances, God is never far away; He is here . . . always right here. So pray.

A person with no devotional life generally struggles with faith and obedience.

—

CHARLES STANLEY

MORE FROM GOD'S WORD ABOUT
WORSHIPPING GOD EVERY DAY

Teach me Your way, Lord, and I will live by Your truth. Give me an undivided mind to fear Your name.

PSALM 86:11 HCSB

I will instruct you and show you the way to go; with My eye on you, I will give counsel.

PSALM 32:8 HCSB

Happy is the man who finds wisdom, and the man who gains understanding.

PROVERBS 3:13 NKJV

But grow in the grace and knowledge of our Lord and Savior Jesus Christ. To Him be the glory both now and to the day of eternity.

2 PETER 3:18 HCSB

In all your ways acknowledge Him, and He shall direct your paths.

PROVERBS 3:6 NKJV

MORE POWERFUL IDEAS ABOUT
YOUR DAILY DEVOTIONAL

Every morning God gives us the gift of comprehending anew His faithfulness of old; thus in the midst of our life with God, we may daily begin a new life with Him.

DIETRICH BONHOEFFER

Jesus challenges you and me to keep our focus daily on the cross of His will if we want to be His disciples.

ANNE GRAHAM LOTZ

I suggest you discipline yourself to spend time daily in a systematic reading of God's Word. Make this "quiet time" a priority that nobody can change.

WARREN WIERSBE

Think of this—we may live together with Him here and now, a daily walking with Him who loved us and gave Himself for us.

ELISABETH ELLIOT

A TIP FOR TODAY

A daily devotional is especially important during those times of your life when you're feeling discouraged, fearful, or stressed.

A PRAYER FOR TODAY

Dear Lord, help me to hear Your direction for my life in the solitary moments that I spend with You. And as I fulfill my responsibilities throughout the day, let my actions and my thoughts be pleasing to You. Amen

TODAY'S THOUGHTS

My thoughts about the importance of spending time with God every morning.

_____

_____

_____

_____

_____

_____

_____

_____

DAY 12

THE RIGHT KIND OF ATTITUDE

For God has not given us a spirit of fearfulness,
but one of power, love,
and sound judgment.

—

2 TIMOTHY 1:7 HCSB

Attitude is more important than the past,
than education, than money, than circumstances,
than what people do or say. It is more important than
appearance, giftedness, or skill.

—

CHARLES SWINDOLL

If you want to build a better future for yourself and your family, you need the right kind of attitude: the positive kind. So what's your attitude today? Are you fearful, angry, bored, or worried? Are you pessimistic, perplexed, pained, and perturbed? Are you moping around with a frown on your face that's almost as big as the one in your heart? If so, God wants to have a little talk with you.

God created you in His own image, and He wants you to experience joy, contentment, peace, and abundance. But, God will not force you to experience these things; you must claim them for yourself.

God has given you free will, including the ability to influence the direction and the tone of your thoughts. And, here's how God wants you to direct those thoughts:

Finally brothers, whatever is true, whatever is honorable, whatever is just, whatever is pure, whatever is lovely, whatever is commendable—if there is any moral excellence and if there is any praise—dwell on these things." (Philippians 4:8 HCSB)

The quality of your attitude will help determine the quality of your life, so you must guard your thoughts accordingly. If you make up your mind to approach life with a healthy mixture of realism and optimism, you'll be rewarded. But, if you allow yourself to fall into the unfortunate habit of negative thinking, you will doom yourself to unhappiness, or mediocrity, or worse.

So, the next time you find yourself dwelling upon the negative aspects of your life, refocus your attention on things positive. The next time you find yourself falling prey to the blight of pessimism, stop yourself and turn your thoughts around. The next time you're tempted to waste valuable time gossiping or complaining, resist those temptations with all your might.

And remember: you'll never whine your way to the top . . . so don't waste your breath.

FOLLOW HIS LEAD

God promises that He has the power to transform your life if you invite Him to do so. Your decision, then, is straightforward: whether or not to allow the Father's transforming power to work in you and through you.

God stands at the door of your heart and waits; all you must do is invite Him in. When you do so, you cannot remain unchanged.

Is there some aspect of your life you'd like to change—a bad habit, an unhealthy relationship, or a missed opportunity? Then ask God to change your attitude and guide your path. Talk specifically to your Creator about the person you are today and the person you want to become tomorrow. When you sincerely petition the Father, you'll be amazed at the things that He and you, working together, can accomplish.

Your attitude is more important than your aptitude.

—

ZIG ZIGLAR

MORE FROM GOD'S WORD ABOUT
YOUR ATTITUDE

Set your mind on things above, not on things on the earth.

COLOSSIANS 3:2 NKJV

Come near to God, and God will come near to you. You sinners, clean sin out of your lives. You who are trying to follow God and the world at the same time, make your thinking pure.

JAMES 4:8 NCV

Those who are pure in their thinking are happy, because they will be with God.

MATTHEW 5:8 NCV

In everything give thanks; for this is the will of God in Christ Jesus for you.

1 THESSALONIANS 5:18 NKJV

Worship the Lord with gladness. Come before him, singing with joy. Acknowledge that the Lord is God! He made us, and we are his. We are his people, the sheep of his pasture.

PSALM 100:2-3 NLT

MORE POWERFUL IDEAS ABOUT
THE IMPORTANCE OF A POSITIVE ATTITUDE

We are either the masters or the victims of our attitudes. It is a matter of personal choice. Who we are today is the result of choices we made yesterday. Tomorrow, we will become what we choose today. To change means to choose to change.

JOHN MAXWELL

The mind is like a clock that is constantly running down. It has to be wound up daily with good thoughts.

FULTON J. SHEEN

Pain is inevitable, but misery is optional.

MAX LUCADO

A TIP FOR TODAY

A positive attitude leads to positive re-sults. If you want to improve the quality of your thoughts, ask God to help you.

The difference between winning and losing is how we choose to react to disappointment.

BARBARA JOHNSON

A PRAYER FOR TODAY

Lord, I pray for an attitude that is Christlike. Whatever my circumstances, whether good or bad, triumphal or tragic, let my response reflect a God-honoring attitude of optimism, faith, and love for You. Amen

TODAY'S THOUGHTS

My thoughts about the importance of maintaining a positive outlook on my life and my future.

_____

_____

_____

_____

_____

_____

_____

_____

_____

DAY 13

DON'T GIVE UP!

No matter how many times you trip them up,
God-loyal people don't stay down long;
Soon they're up on their feet,
while the wicked end up flat on their faces.

—

PROVERBS 24:16 MSG

We don't give up. We look up. We trust. We believe.
And our optimism is not hollow.
Christ has proven worthy.
He has shown that He never fails.
That's what makes God, God.

—

MAX LUCADO

The old saying is as true today as it was when it was first spoken: "Life is a marathon, not a sprint." That's why wise travelers (like you) select a traveling companion who never tires and never falters. That partner, of course, is your Heavenly Father.

The next time you find your courage tested by an unwelcome change, remember that God is as near as your next breath, and remember that He offers strength and comfort to His children. He is your shield and your strength; He is your protector and your deliverer. Call upon Him in your hour of need and then be comforted. Whatever your challenge, whatever your trouble, God can help you persevere. And that's precisely what He'll do if you ask Him.

Perhaps you are in a hurry for God to help you resolve your challenges. Perhaps you're anxious to earn the rewards that you feel you've already earned from life. Perhaps you're drumming your fingers, impatiently waiting for God to act. If so, be forewarned: God operates on His own timetable, not yours. Sometimes, God may answer your prayers with silence, and when He does, you must patiently persevere. In times of trouble, you must remain steadfast and trust in the merciful goodness of your Heavenly Father. Whatever your problem, He can handle it. Your job is to keep persevering until He does.

LOOK TO JESUS

In a world filled with roadblocks and stumbling blocks, we need strength, courage, and perseverance. And, as an example of perfect perseverance, we need look no further than our Savior, Jesus Christ.

Jesus finished what He began. Despite the torture He endured, despite the shame of the cross, Jesus was steadfast in His faithfulness to God. We, too, must remain faithful, especially during times of hardship.

As you navigate the inevitable changes of modern-day life, you will undoubtedly experience your fair share of disappointments, detours, false starts, and failures. When you do, don't become discouraged: God's not finished with you yet.

MORE FROM GOD'S WORD ABOUT
PERSEVERANCE

Let us not become weary in doing good, for at the proper time we will reap a harvest if we do not give up.

GALATIANS 6:9 NIV

For you have need of endurance, so that when you have done the will of God, you may receive what was promised.

HEBREWS 10:36 NASB

Thanks be to God! He gives us the victory through our Lord Jesus Christ. Therefore, my dear brothers, stand firm. Let nothing move you. Always give yourselves fully to the work of the Lord, because you know that your labor in the Lord is not in vain.

1 CORINTHIANS 15:57-58 NIV

Be diligent that ye may be found of him in peace, without spot, and blameless.

2 PETER 3:14 KJV

It is better to finish something than to start it. It is better to be patient than to be proud.

ECCLESIASTES 7:8 NCV

MORE POWERFUL IDEAS ABOUT PERSEVERANCE

As we wait on God, He helps us use the winds of adversity to soar above our problems. As the Bible says, "Those who wait on the LORD . . . shall mount up with wings like eagles."

BILLY GRAHAM

You cannot persevere unless there is a trial in your life. There can be no victories without battles; there can be no peaks without valleys. If you want the blessing, you must be prepared to carry the burden and fight the battle. God has to balance privileges with responsibilities, blessings with burdens, or else you and I will become spoiled, pampered children.

WARREN WIERSBE

A TIP FOR TODAY

If things don't work out at first, don't quit. If you don't keep trying, you'll never know how good you can be.

Failure is one of life's most powerful teachers. How we handle our failures determines whether we're going to simply "get by" in life or "press on."

BETH MOORE

A PRAYER FOR TODAY

Lord, when life is difficult, I am tempted to abandon hope in the future. But You are my God, and I can draw strength from You. Let me trust You, Father, in good times and in bad times. Let me persevere—even if my soul is troubled—and let me follow Your Son, Jesus Christ, this day and forever. Amen

TODAY'S THOUGHTS

My thoughts about the power of perseverance.

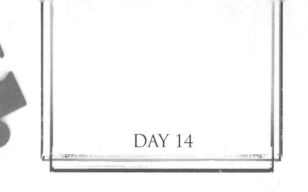

DAY 14

CONSIDER
THE POSSIBILITIES

For nothing will be impossible with God.

—

LUKE 1:37 HCSB

Man's adversity is God's opportunity.

—

MATTHEW HENRY

As you think about ways to manage change and embrace it, don't put limitations on God. He has the power to do miraculous things with you and through you . . . if you let Him.

Are you afraid to ask God to do big things—or to make big changes—in your life? Is your faith threadbare and worn? If so, it's time to abandon your doubts and re-claim your faith in God's promises.

Ours is a God of infinite possibilities. But sometimes, because of limited faith and limited understanding, we wrongly assume that God cannot or will not intervene in the affairs of mankind. Such assumptions are simply wrong.

God's Holy Word makes it clear: absolutely nothing is impossible for the Lord. And since the Bible means what it says, you can be comforted in the knowledge that the Cre-ator of the universe can do miraculous things in your own life and in the lives of your loved ones. Your challenge, as a believer, is to take God at His word, and to expect the miraculous.

OPPORTUNITIES EVERYWHERE

As you look at the landscape of your life, do you see opportunities, possibilities, and blessings, or do you focus, instead, upon the more negative scenery? Do you spend more time counting your blessings or your misfortunes? If you've acquired the unfortunate habit of focusing too intently upon the negative aspects of life, then your spiritual vision is in need of correction.

Whether you realize it or not, opportunities are whirling around you like stars crossing the night sky: beautiful to observe, but too numerous to count. Yet you may be too concerned with the challenges of everyday living to notice those opportunities. That's why you should slow down occasionally, catch your breath, and focus your thoughts on two things: the talents God has given you and the opportunities that He has placed before you. God is leading you in the direction of those opportunities. Your task is to watch carefully, to pray fervently, and to act accordingly.

MORE FROM GOD'S WORD ABOUT POSSIBILITIES

Let us not lose heart in doing good, for in due time we shall reap if we do not grow weary. So then, while we have opportunity, let us do good to all men, and especially to those who are of the household of the faith.

GALATIANS 6:9-10 NASB

Make the most of every opportunity.

COLOSSIANS 4:5 NIV

God is our refuge and strength, a helper who is always found in times of trouble.

PSALM 46:1 HCSB

Dear brothers and sisters, whenever trouble comes your way, let it be an opportunity for joy. For when your faith is tested, your endurance has a chance to grow. So let it grow, for when your endurance is fully developed, you will be strong in character and ready for anything.

JAMES 1:2-4 NLT

93

MORE POWERFUL IDEAS ABOUT POSSIBILITIES

Often God shuts a door in our face so that he can open the door through which he wants us to go.

CATHERINE MARSHALL

Allow your dreams a place in your prayers and plans. God-given dreams can help you move into the future He is preparing for you.

BARBARA JOHNSON

When God is involved, anything can happen. Be open and stay that way. God has a beautiful way of bringing good vibrations out of broken chords.

CHARLES SWINDOLL

A TIP FOR TODAY

Don't invest large quantities of your life focusing on past misfortunes. On the road of life, regret is a dead end.

God specializes in taking tragedy and turning it into triumph. The greater the tragedy, the greater the potential for triumph.

CHARLES STANLEY

A PRAYER FOR TODAY

Dear Lord, give me the courage to dream and the faithfulness to trust in Your perfect plan for my life. When I am worried, give me strength for today and hope for tomorrow. Today, Father, I will trust You and honor You with my thoughts, with my prayers, with my actions, and with my dreams. Amen

TODAY'S THOUGHTS

My thoughts about the miraculous things God has done in the past, and the miraculous things He can do today.

_____

_____

_____

_____

_____

_____

_____

_____

_____

SELF-ESTEEM
ACCORDING TO GOD

For you made us only a little lower than God,
and you crowned us with glory and honor.

—

PSALM 8:5 NLT

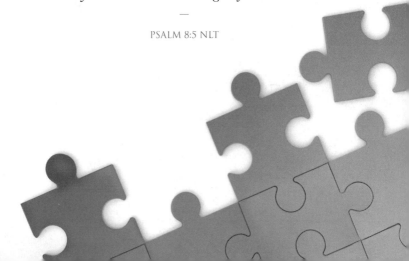

Being loved by Him whose opinion
matters most gives us the security to risk loving, too—
even loving ourselves.

—

GLORIA GAITHER

When you encounter tough times, you may lose self-confidence. Or you may become so focused on what other people are thinking—or saying—that you fail to focus on God. To do so is a mistake of major proportions—don't make it. Instead, seek God's guidance as you focus your energies on becoming the best you that you can possibly be. And when it comes to matters of self-esteem and self-image, seek approval not from your peers, but from your Creator.

Millions of words have been written about various ways to improve self-image and increase self-esteem. Yet, maintaining a healthy self-image is, to a surprising extent, a matter of doing three things: 1. Obeying God, 2. Thinking healthy thoughts, 3. Finding a purpose for your life that pleases your Creator and yourself. The following common-sense, Biblically-based tips can help you build the kind of self-image—and the kind of life—that both you and God can be proud of:

1. Do the right thing: If you're misbehaving, how can you possibly hope to feel good about yourself? (Romans 14:12)

2. Watch what you think: If your inner voice is, in reality, your inner critic, you need to tone down the criticism now. And while you're at it, train yourself to begin thinking thoughts that are more rational, more accepting, and less judgmental. (Philippians 4:8)

3. Spend time with boosters, not critics: Are your friends putting you down? If so, find new friends. (Hebrews 3:13)

4. Don't be a perfectionist: Strive for excellence, but never confuse it with perfection. (Ecclesiastes 11:4,6)

5. If you're addicted to something unhealthy, stop; if you can't stop, get help: Addictions, of whatever type, create havoc in your life. And disorder. And grief. And low self-esteem. (Exodus 20:3)

6. Find a purpose for your life that is larger than you are: When you're dedicated to something or someone besides yourself, you blossom. (Ephesians 6:7)

7. Don't worry too much about self-esteem: Instead, worry more about living a life that is pleasing to God. Learn to think optimistically. Find a worthy purpose. Find people to love and people to serve. When you do, your self-esteem will, on most days, take care of itself.

MORE FROM GOD'S WORD ABOUT
YOUR SELF-WORTH

You're blessed when you're content with just who you are—no more, no less. That's the moment you find yourselves proud owners of everything that can't be bought.

MATTHEW 5:5 MSG

A devout life does bring wealth, but it's the rich simplicity of being yourself before God.

1 TIMOTHY 6:6 MSG

My dear children, let's not just talk about love; let's practice real love. This is the only way we'll know we're living truly, living in God's reality. It's also the way to shut down debilitating self-criticism, even when there is something to it. For God is greater than our worried hearts and knows more about us than we do ourselves. And friends, once that's taken care of and we're no longer accusing or condemning ourselves, we're bold and free before God!

1 JOHN 3:18-21 MSG

To acquire wisdom is to love oneself; people who cherish understanding will prosper.

PROVERBS 19:8 NLT

MORE POWERFUL IDEAS ABOUT
YOUR SELF-WORTH

As you and I lay up for ourselves living, lasting treasures in Heaven, we come to the awesome conclusion that we ourselves are His treasure!

ANNE GRAHAM LOTZ

The Creator has made us each one of a kind. There is nobody else exactly like us, and there never will be. Each of us is his special creation and is alive for a distinctive purpose.

LUCI SWINDOLL

Comparison is the root of all feelings of inferiority.

JAMES DOBSON

A TIP FOR TODAY

No matter the size of your challenges, you can be sure that you and God, working together, can tackle them.

When it comes to our position before God, we're perfect. When he sees each of us, he sees one who has been made perfect through the One who is perfect—Jesus Christ.

MAX LUCADO

A PRAYER FOR TODAY

Dear Lord, help me speak courteously to everyone, including myself. And when I make a mistake, help me to forgive myself quickly and thoroughly, just as I forgive others. Amen

TODAY'S THOUGHTS

My thoughts about the importance of maintaining a positive self-image and an optimistic outlook on life.

_____

_____

_____

_____

_____

_____

_____

_____

_____

_____

DAY 16

KEEPING POSSESSIONS IN PERSPECTIVE

Don't collect for yourselves treasures on earth,
where moth and rust destroy and where thieves break
in and steal. But collect for yourselves treasures in
heaven, where neither moth nor rust destroys,
and where thieves don't break in and steal.
For where your treasure is,
there your heart will be also.

—

MATTHEW 6:19-21 HCSB

A society that pursues pleasure runs the risk of raising
expectations ever higher, so that true contentment
always lies tantalizingly out of reach.

—

PHILIP YANCEY AND PAUL BRAND

All too often we focus our thoughts and energies on the accumulation of earthly treasures, creating untold stress in our lives and leaving precious little time to accumulate the only treasures that really matter: the spiritual kind. Our material possessions have the potential to do great good—depending upon how we use them. If we allow the things we own to own us, we may pay dearly for our misplaced priorities.

Society focuses intently on material possessions, but God's Word teaches us time and again that money matters little when compared to the spiritual gifts that the Creator offers to those who put Him first in their lives. So today, keep your possessions in perspective. Remember that God should come first, and everything else next. When you give God His rightful place in your heart, you'll have a clearer vision of the things that really matter. Then, you can joyfully thank your Heavenly Father for spiritual blessings that are, in truth, too numerous to count.

BEWARE OF BECOMING TOO FRIENDLY WITH THE WORLD

We live in the world, but we must not worship it. Our duty is to place God first and everything else second. But because we are fallible beings with imperfect faith, placing God in His rightful place is often difficult. In fact, at every turn, or so it seems, we are tempted to do otherwise.

The 21st-century world is a noisy, distracting place filled with countless opportunities to stray from God's will. The world seems to cry, "Worship me with your time, your money, your energy, and your thoughts!" But God commands otherwise: He commands us to worship Him and Him alone; everything else must be secondary.

Outside appearances, things like the clothes you wear or the car you drive, are important to other people but totally unimportant to God. Trust God.

—

MARIE T. FREEMAN

MORE FROM GOD'S WORD ABOUT MATERIALISM

And He told them, "Watch out and be on guard against all greed, because one's life is not in the abundance of his possessions."

LUKE 12:15 HCSB

For what does it benefit a man to gain the whole world yet lose his life? What can a man give in exchange for his life?

MARK 8:36-37 HCSB

Anyone trusting in his riches will fall, but the righteous will flourish like foliage.

PROVERBS 11:28 HCSB

Put on the whole armor of God, that you may be able to stand against the wiles of the devil.

EPHESIANS 6:11 NKJV

The Lord knows how to deliver the godly out of temptations.

2 PETER 2:9 NKJV

MORE POWERFUL IDEAS ABOUT
THE DANGERS OF MATERIALISM

Greed is enslaving. The more you have, the more you want—until eventually avarice consumes you.

KAY ARTHUR

It's sobering to contemplate how much time, effort, sacrifice, compromise, and attention we give to acquiring and increasing our supply of something that is totally insignificant in eternity.

ANNE GRAHAM LOTZ

As faithful stewards of what we have, ought we not to give earnest thought to our staggering surplus?

ELISABETH ELLIOT

A TIP FOR TODAY

Material possessions may seem appealing at first, but they pale in comparison to the spiritual gifts that God gives to those who put Him first.

If you want to be truly happy, you won't find it on an endless quest for more stuff. You'll find it in receiving God's generosity and then passing that generosity along.

BILL HYBELS

A PRAYER FOR TODAY

Dear Lord, when I focus on the world's messages, I suffer. But, when I focus on Your message, I am blessed. Direct me far from the distractions of this world, and let me follow in the footsteps of Your Son today and forever. Amen

TODAY'S THOUGHTS

My thoughts about the dangers of materialism.

_____

_____

_____

_____

_____

_____

_____

_____

_____

_____

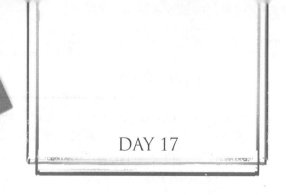

DAY 17

NO PROBLEMS ARE
TOO BIG FOR GOD

Is anything too hard for the LORD?

—

GENESIS 18:14 KJV

Underneath each trouble there is a faithful purpose.

C. H. SPURGEON

H ere's a riddle: What is it that is too unimportant to pray about yet too big for God to handle? The answer, of course, is: "nothing." Yet sometimes, when the challenges of the day seem overwhelming, we may spend more time worrying about our troubles than praying about them. And, we may spend more time fretting about our problems than solving them. A far better strategy, of course, is to pray as if everything depended entirely upon God and to work as if everything depended entirely upon us.

Life is an exercise in problem-solving. The question is not whether we will encounter problems; the real question is how we will choose to address them. When it comes to solving the problems of everyday living, we often know precisely what needs to be done, but we may be slow in doing it—especially if what needs to be done is difficult or uncomfortable for us. So we put off till tomorrow what should be done today.

The words of Psalm 34 remind us that the Lord solves problems for "people who do what is right." And usually, "doing what is right" means doing the uncomfortable work of confronting our problems sooner rather than later.

DO SOMETHING TODAY

Perhaps your troubles are simply too big to solve in a single sitting. But just because you can't solve everything doesn't mean that you should do nothing. So today, as a favor to yourself and as a way of breaking the bonds of procrastination, do something to make your situation better. Even a small step in the right direction is still a step in the right direction. And a small step is far, far better than no step at all.

The grace of God is sufficient for all our needs,
for every problem and for every difficulty,
for every broken heart,
and for every human sorrow.

—

PETER MARSHALL

MORE FROM GOD'S WORD ABOUT PROBLEMS

People who do what is right may have many problems, but the Lord will solve them all.

PSALM 34:19 NCV

For when the way is rough, your patience has a chance to grow. So let it grow, and don't try to squirm out of your problems.

JAMES 1:3-4 TLB

When you go through deep waters and great trouble, I will be with you. When you go through the rivers of difficulty, you will not drown! When you walk through the fire of oppression, you will not be burned up; the flames will not consume you. For I am the Lord, your God . . .

ISAIAH 43:2-3 NLT

Come to me, all you who are weary and burdened, and I will give you rest. Take my yoke upon you and learn from me, for I am gentle and humble in heart, and you will find rest for your souls. For my yoke is easy and my burden is light.

MATTHEW 11:28-30 NIV

MORE POWERFUL IDEAS ABOUT
OVERCOMING CHALLENGES

God knows exactly how much you can take, and He will never permit you to reach a breaking point.

BARBARA JOHNSON

Measure the size of the obstacles against the size of God.

BETH MOORE

Troubles we bear trustfully can bring us a fresh vision of God and a new outlook on life, an outlook of peace and hope.

BILLY GRAHAM

A TIP FOR TODAY

When it comes to solving your problems, work beats worry. Remember: it is better to fix than to fret.

We must face today as children of tomorrow. We must meet the uncertainties of this world with the certainty of the world to come. To the pure in heart nothing really bad can happen...not death, but sin, should be our greatest fear.

A. W. TOZER

A PRAYER FOR TODAY

Lord, sometimes my problems are simply too big for me, but they are never too big for You. Let me turn my troubles over to You, Lord, and let me trust in You today and for all eternity. Amen

TODAY'S THOUGHTS

My thoughts about an important challenge I need to address today.

_____

_____

_____

_____

_____

_____

_____

_____

_____

DAY 18

DEFEATING PROCRASTINATION

*If you wait for perfect conditions,
you will never get anything done.*

—

ECCLESIASTES 11:4 NLT

Not now becomes never.

—

MARTIN LUTHER

When life's inevitable changes seem overwhelming, it's easy (and tempting) to avoid those hard-to-do tasks that you would prefer to avoid altogether. But the habit of procrastination takes a double toll: first, important work goes unfinished, and second, valuable energy is wasted in the process of putting off the things that remain undone.

God has created a world that punishes procrastinators and rewards men and women who "do it now." In other words, life doesn't procrastinate. Neither should you. So if you've been putting things off instead of getting things done, here are some things you can do:

1. Have a clear understanding of your short and long term goals, and set your priorities in accordance with those goals.

2. When faced with distasteful tasks, do them immediately, preferably first thing in the morning (even if the unpleasantness is a low-priority activity, go ahead and get it out of the way if it can be completed quickly). Dispatching distasteful tasks sooner rather than later will improve the quality of your day and prevent you from wasting un-

told amounts of energy in the process of fighting against yourself.

3. Avoid the trap of perfectionism. Be willing to do your best, and be satisfied with the results.

4. If you don't already own one, purchase a daily or weekly planning system that fits your needs. If used properly, a planning calendar is worth many times what you pay for it.

5. Start each work day with a clear written "to-do" list, ranked according to importance. At lunch time, take a moment to collect your thoughts, reexamine your list, and refocus your efforts on the most important things you wish to accomplish during the remainder of the day.

DON'T BE AFRAID TO START SMALL

Perhaps your troubles are simply too big to solve in a single sitting. But just because you can't solve everything doesn't mean that you should do nothing. So today, as a favor to yourself and as a way of breaking the bonds of procrastination, do something to make your situation better. Even a small step in the right direction is still a step in the right direction. And a small step is far, far better than no step at all.

MORE FROM GOD'S WORD ABOUT
PROCRASTINATION

If you do nothing in a difficult time, your strength is limited.

PROVERBS 24:10 HCSB

If you are too lazy to plow in the right season, you will have no food at the harvest.

PROVERBS 20:4 NLT

When you make a vow to God, do not delay in fulfilling it. He has no pleasure in fools; fulfill your vow.

ECCLESIASTES 5:4 NIV

We can't afford to waste a minute, must not squander these precious daylight hours in frivolity and indulgence, in sleeping around and dissipation, in bickering and grabbing everything in sight. Get out of bed and get dressed! Don't loiter and linger, waiting until the very last minute. Dress yourselves in Christ, and be up and about!

ROMANS 13:13-14 MSG

Whatever you do, do it enthusiastically, as something done for the Lord and not for men.

COLOSSIANS 3:23 HCSB

MORE POWERFUL IDEAS ABOUT PROCRASTINATION

I've found that the worst thing I can do when it comes to any kind of potential pressure situation is to put off dealing with it.

JOHN MAXWELL

Do noble things, do not dream them all day long.

CHARLES KINGSLEY

Do not build up obstacles in your imagination. Difficulties must be studied and dealt with, but they must not be magnified by fear.

NORMAN VINCENT PEALE

A TIP FOR TODAY

The habit of procrastination is often rooted in the fear of failure or the fear of embarrassment. Your challenge is to confront these fears and defeat them.

Never confuse activity with productivity.

RICK WARREN

I cannot fix what I will not face.

JIM GALLERY

A PRAYER FOR TODAY

Dear Lord, when I am confronted with things that need to be done, give me the courage and the wisdom to do them now, not later. Amen

TODAY'S THOUGHTS

My thoughts about an important challenge that I've been avoiding.

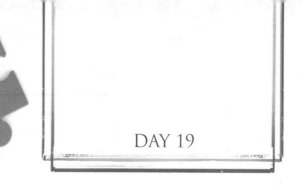

DAY 19

LIVE COURAGEOUSLY

*They do not fear bad news; they confidently trust
the Lord to care for them. They are confident and
fearless and can face their foes triumphantly.*

—

PSALM 112:7-8 NLT

Faith not only can help you through a crisis, it can help you to approach life after the hard times with a whole new perspective. It can help you adopt an outlook of hope and courage through faith to face reality.

—

JOHN MAXWELL

Every person's life is a tapestry of events: some wonderful, some not-so-wonderful, and some downright disastrous. When we visit the mountaintops of life, praising God isn't hard—in fact, it's easy. In our moments of triumph, we can bow our heads and thank God for our victories. But when we fail to reach the mountaintops, when we endure the inevitable losses that are a part of every person's life, we find it much tougher to give God the praise He deserves. Yet wherever we find ourselves, whether on the mountaintops of life or in life's darkest valleys, we must still offer thanks to God, giving thanks in all circumstances.

The next time you find yourself worried about the challenges of today or the uncertainties of tomorrow, ask yourself this question: Are you really ready to place your concerns and your life in God's all-powerful, all-knowing, all-loving hands? If the answer to that question is yes—as it should be—then you can draw courage today from the source of strength that never fails: your Father in heaven.

God is not a distant being. He is not absent from our world, nor is He absent from your world. God is not "out there"; He is "right here," continuously reshaping His universe, and continuously reshaping the lives of those who dwell in it.

God is with you always, listening to your thoughts and prayers, watching over your every move. If the demands of everyday life weigh down upon you, you may be tempted to ignore God's presence or—worse yet—to lose faith in His promises. But, when you quiet yourself and acknowledge His presence, God will touch your heart and restore your courage.

At this very moment—as you're fulfilling your obligations and overcoming tough times—God is seeking to work in you and through you. He's asking you to live abundantly and courageously . . . and He's ready to help. So why not let Him do it . . . starting now?

Do not let Satan deceive you into being afraid
of God's plans for your life.

—

R. A. TORREY

MORE FROM GOD'S WORD ABOUT COURAGE

Be strong and courageous, and do the work. Don't be afraid or discouraged by the size of the task, for the LORD God, my God, is with you. He will not fail you or forsake you.

1 CHRONICLES 28:20 NLT

Therefore, being always of good courage . . . we walk by faith, not by sight.

2 CORINTHIANS 5:6-7 NASB

God doesn't want us to be shy with his gifts, but bold and loving and sensible.

2 TIMOTHY 1:7 MSG

The LORD himself goes before you and will be with you; he will never leave you nor forsake you. Do not be afraid; do not be discouraged.

DEUTERONOMY 31:8 NIV

But Moses said to the people, "Do not fear! Stand by and see the salvation of the LORD."

EXODUS 14:13 NASB

MORE POWERFUL IDEAS ABOUT COURAGE

Seeing that a Pilot steers the ship in which we sail, who will never allow us to perish even in the midst of shipwrecks, there is no reason why our minds should be overwhelmed with fear and overcome with weariness.

JOHN CALVIN

Like dynamite, God's power is only latent power until it is released. You can release God's dynamite power into people's lives and into the world through faith, through words, and through prayer.

BILL BRIGHT

Faith is stronger than fear.

JOHN MAXWELL

A TIP FOR TODAY

With God as your partner, you can handle absolutely anything that comes your way. When you sincerely turn to Him, He will never fail you.

Jesus Christ can make the weakest man into a divine dreadnought, fearing nothing.

OSWALD CHAMBERS

A PRAYER FOR TODAY

Lord, sometimes I face challenges that leave me breathless. When I am fearful, let me lean upon You. Keep me ever mindful, Lord, that You are my God, my strength, and my shield. With You by my side, I have nothing to fear. And, with Your Son, Jesus, as my Savior, I have received the priceless gift of eternal life. Help me to be a grateful and courageous servant this day and every day. Amen

TODAY'S THOUGHTS

My thoughts about trusting God to lead me through and beyond today's challenges.

DAY 20

DON'T WORRY: YOU'RE NEVER ALONE

The Lord is the One who will go before you.
He will be with you;
He will not leave you or forsake you.
Do not be afraid or discouraged.

—

DEUTERONOMY 31:8 HCSB

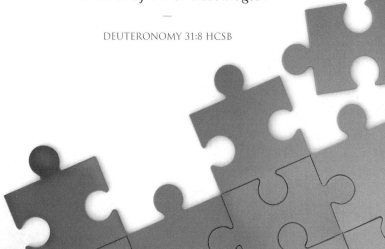

Get yourself into the presence of the loving Father.
Just place yourself before Him, and look up into, His face;
think of His love, His wonderful, tender, pitying love.

—

ANDREW MURRAY

I f God is everywhere, why does He sometimes seem so far away? The answer to that question, of course, has nothing to do with God and everything to do with us.

When we begin each day on our knees, in praise and worship to Him, God often seems very near indeed. But, if we ignore God's presence or—worse yet—rebel against it altogether, the world in which we live becomes a spiritual wasteland.

Are you tired, discouraged, or fearful? Be comforted because God is with you. Are you confused? Listen to the quiet voice of your Heavenly Father. Are you bitter? Talk with God and seek His guidance. Are you celebrating a great victory? Thank God and praise Him. He is the Giver of all things good.

In whatever condition you find yourself, wherever you are, whether you are happy or sad, victorious or vanquished, troubled or triumphant, celebrate God's presence. And be comforted. God is not just near. He is here.

SPENDING QUIET MOMENTS WITH GOD

We live in an ever-changing, fast-paced world. The demands of everyday life can seem overwhelming at times, but when we slow ourselves down and seek the presence of a loving God, we invite His peace into our hearts.

Do you set aside quiet moments each day to offer praise to your Creator? You should. During these moments of stillness, you will often sense the infinite love and power of our Lord.

The familiar words of Psalm 46:10 remind us to "be still, and know that I am God" (NIV). When we do so, we encounter the awesome presence of our loving Heavenly Father, and we are comforted in the knowledge that God is not just near. He is here.

> God is in the midst of whatever has happened,
> is happening, and will happen.
>
> —
>
> CHARLES SWINDOLL

MORE FROM GOD'S WORD ABOUT
HIS PRESENCE

Come near to God, and God will come near to you. You sinners, clean sin out of your lives. You who are trying to follow God and the world at the same time, make your thinking pure.

JAMES 4:8 NCV

Again, this is God's command: to believe in his personally named Son, Jesus Christ. He told us to love each other, in line with the original command. As we keep his commands, we live deeply and surely in him, and he lives in us. And this is how we experience his deep and abiding presence in us: by the Spirit he gave us.

1 JOHN 3:23-24 MSG

For the eyes of the Lord range throughout the earth to strengthen those whose hearts are fully committed to him.

2 CHRONICLES 16:9 NIV

God did this so that men would seek him and perhaps reach out for him and find him, though he is not far from each one of us.

ACTS 17:27 NIV

MORE POWERFUL IDEAS ABOUT
GOD'S PRESENCE

God's silence is in no way indicative of His activity or involvement in our lives. He may be silent, but He is not still.

CHARLES SWINDOLL

We should learn to live in the presence of the living God. He should be a well for us: delightful, comforting, unfailing, springing up to eternal life (John 4:14). When we rely on other people, their water supplies ultimately dry up. But, the well of the Creator never fails to nourish us.

C. H. SPURGEON

A TIP FOR TODAY
Listen to God. Slow yourself down, tune out the distractions, and listen carefully. God has important things to say; your task is to be still and listen.

Certainly, God is with us in times of distress, and that is a comforting truth. But listen: Jesus wants to be part of every experience and every moment of our lives.

BILLY GRAHAM

A PRAYER FOR TODAY

Heavenly Father, even when it seems to me that You are far away, You never leave my side. Today and every day, I will strive to feel Your presence, and I will strive to sense Your love for me. Amen

TODAY'S THOUGHTS

My thoughts about the importance of finding quiet time each day to sense God's presence and His love.

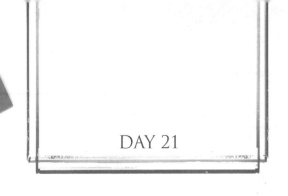

DAY 21

BE THANKFUL AND WORSHIP HIM

*Therefore as you have received Christ Jesus
the Lord, walk in Him, rooted and built up in Him
and established in the faith, just as you were taught,
and overflowing with thankfulness.*

—

COLOSSIANS 2:6-7 HCSB

It is always possible to be thankful for what is given
rather than to complain about what is not given.
One or the other becomes a habit of life.

—

ELISABETH ELLIOT

As believing Christians, we are blessed beyond measure. God sent His only Son to die for our sins. And, God has given us the priceless gifts of eternal love and eternal life. We, in turn, are instructed to approach our Heavenly Father with reverence and thanksgiving. But sometimes, in the crush of everyday living, we simply don't stop long enough to pause and thank our Creator for the countless blessings He has bestowed upon us.

When we slow down and express our gratitude to the One who made us, we enrich our own lives and the lives of those around us. Thanksgiving should become a habit, a regular part of our daily routines. God has blessed us beyond measure, and we owe Him everything, including our eternal praise.

Are you a thankful person? Do you appreciate the gifts that God has given you? And, do you demonstrate your gratitude by being a faithful steward of the gifts and talents that you have received from your Creator? You most certainly should be thankful. After all, when you stop to think about it, God has given you more blessings than you can count. So the question of the day is this: Will you thank your Heavenly Father . . . or will you spend your time and energy doing other things?

God is always listening—are you willing to say thanks? It's up to you, and the next move is yours.

WORSHIP HIM TODAY

God has a wonderful plan for your life, and an important part of that plan includes worship. We should never deceive ourselves: every life is based upon some form of worship. The question is not whether we worship, but what we worship.

Some of us choose to worship God. The result is a plentiful harvest of joy, peace, and abundance. Others distance themselves from God by foolishly worshiping earthly possessions and personal gratification. To do so is a mistake of profound proportions.

Have you accepted the grace of God's only begotten Son? Then worship Him. Worship Him today and every day. Worship Him with sincerity and thanksgiving. Write His name on your heart and rest assured that He, too, has written your name on His.

MORE FROM GOD'S WORD ABOUT
THANKSGIVING

Thanks be to God for His indescribable gift.

2 CORINTHIANS 9:15 HCSB

And let the peace of the Messiah, to which you were also called in one body, control your hearts. Be thankful.

COLOSSIANS 3:15 HCSB

It is good to give thanks to the Lord, and to sing praises to Your name, O Most High.

PSALM 92:1 NKJV

Praise the Lord! Oh, give thanks to the Lord, for He is good! For His mercy endures forever.

PSALM 106:1 NKJV

In everything give thanks; for this is the will of God in Christ Jesus for you.

2 THESSALONIANS 5:18 NKJV

MORE POWERFUL IDEAS ABOUT
THANKSGIVING

Praise and thank God for who He is and for what He has done for you.

BILLY GRAHAM

The words "thank" and "think" come from the same root word. If we would think more, we would thank more.

WARREN WIERSBE

God often keeps us on the path by guiding us through the counsel of friends and trusted spiritual advisors.

BILL HYBELS

A TIP FOR TODAY

You owe God everything . . . including your thanks.

The act of thanksgiving is a demonstration of the fact that you are going to trust and believe God.

KAY ARTHUR

A PRAYER FOR TODAY

Heavenly Father, let today and every day be a time of worship. Let me worship You, not only with words and deeds, but also with my heart. In the quiet moments of the day, let me praise You and thank You for creating me, loving me, guiding me, and saving me. Amen

TODAY'S THOUGHTS

My thoughts about the many ways God has blessed me and my loved ones.

_____

_____

_____

_____

_____

_____

_____

_____

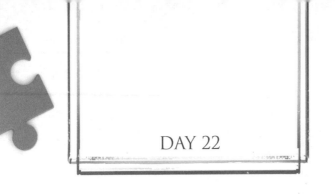

DAY 22

STUDY GOD'S WORD

All Scripture is inspired by God and is profitable for teaching, for rebuking, for correcting, for training in righteousness, so that the man of God may be complete, equipped for every good work.

—

2 TIMOTHY 3:16-17 HCSB

The Bible is God's Word, given to us by God Himself
so we can know Him and His will for our lives.

—

BILLY GRAHAM

The words of Matthew 4:4 remind us that "man shall not live by bread alone but by every word that proceedeth out of the mouth of God" (KJV). As believers, we must study the Bible and meditate upon its meaning for our lives. Otherwise, we deprive ourselves of a priceless gift from our Creator.

God's Word is unlike any other book. The Bible is a road map for life here on earth and for life eternal. As Christians, we are called upon to study God's Holy Word, to follow its commandments, and to share its Good News with the world.

Jonathan Edwards advised, "Be assiduous in reading the Holy Scriptures. This is the fountain whence all knowledge in divinity must be derived. Therefore let not this treasure lie by you neglected." God's Holy Word is, indeed, a priceless, one-of-a-kind treasure, and a passing acquaintance with the Good Book is insufficient for Christians who seek to obey God's Word and to understand His will. After all, man does not live by bread alone . . .

GOD'S WORD REDUCES STRESS

If you're experiencing stress, God's Word can help relieve it. And if you'd like to experience God's peace, Bible study can help provide it.

Warren Wiersbe observed, "When the child of God looks into the Word of God, he sees the Son of God. And, he is transformed by the Spirit of God to share in the glory of God." God's Holy Word is, indeed, a life-changing, stress-reducing, one-of-a-kind treasure. And it's up to you—and only you—to use it that way.

Weave the fabric of God's word through your
heart and mind. It will hold strong,
even if the rest of life unravels.

—

GIGI GRAHAM TCHIVIDJIAN

MORE FROM GOD'S WORD ABOUT HIS WORD

This is my comfort in my affliction, for Your word has given me life.

PSALM 119:50 NKJV

But the word of the Lord endures forever. And this is the word that was preached as the gospel to you.

1 PETER 1:25 HCSB

Let the Word of Christ—the Message—have the run of the house. Give it plenty of room in your lives. Instruct and direct one another using good common sense. And sing, sing your hearts out to God! Let every detail in your lives—words, actions, whatever—be done in the name of the Master, Jesus, thanking God the Father every step of the way.

COLOSSIANS 3:16-17 MSG

For the word of God is living and active. Sharper than any double-edged sword, it penetrates even to dividing soul and spirit, joints and marrow; it judges the thoughts and attitudes of the heart.

HEBREWS 4:12 NIV

MORE POWERFUL IDEAS ABOUT GOD'S WORD

God has given us all sorts of counsel and direction in his written Word; thank God, we have it written down in black and white.

JOHN ELDREDGE

The strength that we claim from God's Word does not depend on circumstances. Circumstances will be difficult, but our strength will be sufficient.

CORRIE TEN BOOM

Nobody ever outgrows Scripture; the book widens and deepens with our years.

C. H. SPURGEON

A TIP FOR TODAY

Take a Bible with you wherever you go. You never know when you may need a midday spiritual pick-me-up.

Prayer and the Word are inseparably linked together. Power in the use of either depends on the presence of the other.

ANDREW MURRAY

A PRAYER FOR TODAY

Heavenly Father, Your Word is a light unto the world; I will study it and trust it and share it. In all that I do, help me be a worthy witness for You as I share the Good News of Your perfect Son and Your perfect Word. Amen

TODAY'S THOUGHTS

My thoughts about the rewards of regular Bible study.

DAY 23

LEARN TO ACCEPT THE THINGS YOU CANNOT CHANGE

*For everything created by God is good,
and nothing should be rejected if it is
received with thanksgiving.*

—

1 TIMOTHY 4:4 HCSB

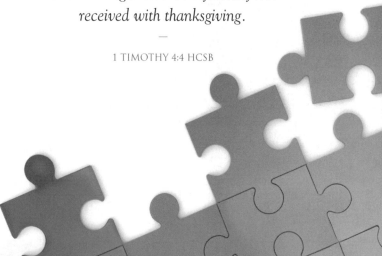

Have courage for the great sorrows of life and patience
for the small ones, and when you have laboriously
accomplished your daily task, go to sleep in peace.
God is awake.

VICTOR HUGO

Are you embittered by an unexpected change or an unwelcome challenge that you did not deserve and cannot understand? If so, it's time to accept the unchangeable past and to have faith in the promise of tomorrow. It's time to trust God completely—and it's time to reclaim the peace—His peace—that can and should be yours.

On occasion, you will be confronted with situations that you simply don't understand. But God does. And He has a reason for everything that He does.

God doesn't explain Himself in ways that we, as mortals with limited insight and clouded vision, can comprehend. So, instead of understanding every aspect of God's unfolding plan for our lives and our universe, we must be satisfied to trust Him completely. We cannot know God's motivations, nor can we understand His actions. We can, however, trust Him, and we must.

WHEN DREAMS DON'T COME TRUE

Some of our most important dreams are the ones we abandon. Some of our most important goals are the ones we don't attain. Sometimes, our most important journeys are the ones that we take to the winding conclusion of what seem to be dead-end streets. Thankfully, with God there are no dead ends; there are only opportunities to learn, to yield, to trust, to serve, and to grow.

The next time you experience one of life's inevitable disappointments, don't despair and don't be afraid to try "Plan B." Consider every setback an opportunity to choose a different, more appropriate path. Have faith that God may indeed be leading you in an entirely different direction, a direction of His choosing. And as you take your next step, remember that what looks like a dead-end to you may, in fact, be the fast lane according to God.

Ultimately things work out best for those
who make the best of the way things work out.

—

BARBARA JOHNSON

MORE FROM GOD'S WORD ABOUT
ACCEPTANCE

A man's heart plans his way, but the Lord determines his steps.

PROVERBS 16:9 HCSB

Do not remember the past events, pay no attention to things of old. Look, I am about to do something new; even now it is coming. Do you not see it? Indeed, I will make a way in the wilderness, rivers in the desert.

ISAIAH 43:18-19 HCSB

Should we accept only good from God and not adversity?

JOB 2:10 HCSB

Come to terms with God and be at peace; in this way good will come to you.

JOB 22:21 HCSB

Sheathe your sword! Should I not drink the cup that the Father has given Me?

JOHN 18:11 HCSB

MORE POWERFUL IDEAS ABOUT ACCEPTANCE

Surrender to the Lord is not a tremendous sacrifice, not an agonizing performance. It is the most sensible thing you can do.

CORRIE TEN BOOM

He does not need to transplant us into a different field. He transforms the very things that were before our greatest hindrances, into the chief and most blessed means of our growth. No difficulties in your case can baffle Him. Put yourself absolutely into His hands, and let Him have His own way with you.

ELISABETH ELLIOT

A TIP FOR TODAY

When we cannot understand God's plan for our lives, we should be thankful for His eternal perspective and His eternal love.

Acceptance is taking from God's hand absolutely anything He gives, looking into His face in trust and thanksgiving, knowing that the confinement of the situation we're in is good and for His glory.

CHARLES SWINDOLL

A PRAYER FOR TODAY

Father, the events of this world unfold according to a plan that I cannot fully understand. But You understand. Help me to trust You, Lord, even when I am grieving. Help me to trust You even when I am confused. Today, in whatever circumstances I find myself, let me trust Your will and accept Your love . . . completely. Amen

TODAY'S THOUGHTS

My thoughts about the things I cannot change.

_____

_____

_____

_____

_____

_____

_____

_____

_____

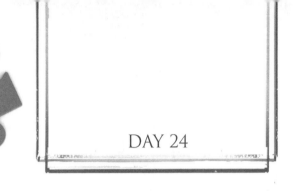

DAY 24

USING YOUR TALENTS

*According to the grace given to us, we have
different gifts: If prophecy, use it according to
the standard of faith; if service, in service;
if teaching, in teaching; if exhorting, in exhortation;
giving, with generosity; leading, with diligence;
showing mercy, with cheerfulness.*

—

ROMANS 12:6-8 HCSB

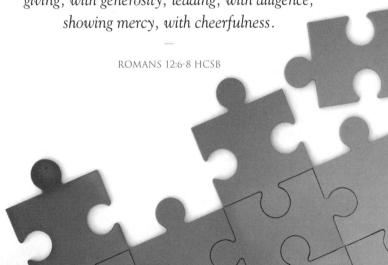

You are a unique blend of talents, skills, and gifts,
which makes you an indispensable member
of the body of Christ.

—

CHARLES STANLEY

God knew precisely what He was doing when He gave you a unique set of talents and opportunities. And now, God wants you to use those talents for the glory of His kingdom. So here's the BIG question: Are you going to use those talents, or not?

Our Heavenly Father instructs us to be faithful stewards of the gifts that He bestows upon us. But we live in a world that encourages us to do otherwise. Ours is a society that is filled to the brim with countless opportunities to squander our time, our resources, and our talents. So we must be watchful for distractions and temptations that might lead us astray.

Every day of your life, you have a choice to make: nurture your talents or neglect them. When you choose wisely, God rewards your efforts, and He expands your opportunities to serve Him.

If you're sincerely interested in building a successful life, build it upon the talents that God (in His infinite wisdom) has given you. Don't try to build a career around the talents you wish He had given you.

In this fast-changing world, God has blessed you with unique opportunities to serve Him. And, He has given you every tool that you need to do so. Today, accept this challenge: value the talent that God has given you, nourish it, make it grow, and share it with the world. After all, the best way to say "Thank You" for God's gifts is to use them.

BE STILL

Ours is a fast-changing world, a world where the demands of the day can seem overwhelming at times. But, when we slow ourselves down and seek the presence of a loving God, we invite His peace into our hearts.

Do you carve out quiet moments each day to offer thanksgiving and praise to your Creator? You should. During these moments of stillness, you will often sense the infinite love and power of our Lord.

Again the familiar words of Psalm 46:10 remind us to "be still, and know that I am God" (NIV). When we do so, we encounter the awesome presence of our loving Heavenly Father, and we are blessed beyond words.

MORE FROM GOD'S WORD ABOUT
USING HIS GIFTS

His master said to him, "Well done, good and faithful slave! You were faithful over a few things; I will put you in charge of many things. Enter your master's joy!"

MATTHEW 25:21 HCSB

Every good gift and every perfect gift is from above, and cometh down from the Father of lights.

JAMES 1:17 KJV

Do not neglect the gift that is in you.

1 TIMOTHY 4:14 HCSB

I remind you to keep ablaze the gift of God that is in you.

2 TIMOTHY 1:6 HCSB

Finally, be strengthened by the Lord and by His vast strength.

EPHESIANS 6:10 HCSB

MORE POWERFUL IDEAS ABOUT YOUR TALENTS

Employ whatever God has entrusted you with, in doing good, all possible good, in every possible kind and degree.

JOHN WESLEY

If you want to reach your potential, you need to add a strong work ethic to your talent.

JOHN MAXWELL

Not everyone possesses boundless energy or a conspicuous talent. We are not equally blessed with great intellect or physical beauty or emotional strength. But we have all been given the same ability to be faithful.

GIGI GRAHAM TCHIVIDJIAN

A TIP FOR TODAY

God has given you a unique array of talents and opportunities. The rest is up to you.

In the great orchestra we call life, you have an instrument and a song, and you owe it to God to play them both sublimely.

MAX LUCADO

A PRAYER FOR TODAY

Lord, You have given all of us talents, and I am no exception. You have blessed me with a gift—let me discover it, nurture it, and use it for the glory of Your kingdom. I will share my gifts with the world, and I will praise You, the Giver of all things good. Amen

TODAY'S THOUGHTS

My thoughts about the importance of discovering—and using—my talents.

_____

_____

_____

_____

_____

_____

_____

_____

DAY 25

THE POWER OF HOPE

I wait for the Lord;
I wait, and put my hope in His word.

—

PSALM 130:5 HCSB

People are genuinely motivated by hope and
a part of that hope is the assurance of future glory
with God for those who are His people.

—

WARREN WIERSBE

There are few sadder sights on earth than the sight of a man or woman who has lost all hope. In difficult times, hope can be elusive, but those who place their faith in God's promises need never lose it. After all, God is good; His love endures; He has promised His children the gift of eternal life. And, God keeps His promises.

Despite God's promises, despite Christ's love, and despite our countless blessings, we frail human beings can still lose hope from time to time. When we do, we need the encouragement of trusted friends, the life-changing power of prayer, and the healing truth of God's Holy Word.

If you find yourself falling into the spiritual traps of worry and discouragement, seek the healing touch of Jesus and the encouraging words of fellow Christians. If you find a friend in need, remind him or her of the peace that is found through a personal relationship with Christ. It was Christ who promised, "These things I have spoken unto you, that in me ye might have peace. In the world ye shall have tribulation: but be of good cheer; I have overcome the world" (John 16:33 KJV). This world can be a place of trials and tribulations, but as believers, we are secure. God has promised us peace, joy, and eternal life. And, of course, God keeps His promises today, tomorrow, and forever.

BE JOYFUL

Have you made the choice to rejoice? Hopefully so. After all, if you're a believer, you have plenty of reasons to be joyful. Yet sometimes, amid the inevitable hustle and bustle of life here on earth, you may lose sight of your blessings as you wrestle with the challenges of everyday life.

Psalm 100 reminds us that, as believers, we have every reason to celebrate: "Shout for joy to the LORD, all the earth. Worship the LORD with gladness" (vv. 1-2 NIV). Yet sometimes, we can forfeit—albeit temporarily—the joy that God intends for our lives.

If you find yourself feeling discouraged or worse, it's time to slow down and have a quiet conversation with your Creator. If your heart is heavy, open the door of your soul to the Father and to His only begotten Son. Christ offers you His peace and His joy. Accept it and share it freely, just as Christ has freely shared His joy with you.

MORE FROM GOD'S WORD ABOUT HOPE

Let us hold on to the confession of our hope without wavering, for He who promised is faithful.

HEBREWS 10:23 HCSB

Hope deferred makes the heart sick.

PROVERBS 13:12 NKJV

Sustain me as You promised, and I will live; do not let me be ashamed of my hope.

PSALM 119:116 HCSB

For I know the thoughts that I think toward you, says the Lord, thoughts of peace and not of evil, to give you a future and a hope. Then you will call upon Me and go and pray to Me, and I will listen to you.

JEREMIAH 29:11-12 NKJV

Be of good courage, and He shall strengthen your heart, all you who hope in the Lord.

PSALM 31:24 NKJV

MORE POWERFUL IDEAS ABOUT HOPE

I wish I could make it all new again; I can't. But God can. "He restores my soul," wrote the shepherd. God doesn't reform; he restores. He doesn't camouflage the old; he restores the new. The Master Builder will pull out the original plan and restore it. He will restore the vigor, he will restore the energy. He will restore the hope. He will restore the soul.

MAX LUCADO

I discovered that sorrow was not to be feared but rather endured with hope and expectancy that God would use it to visit and bless my life.

JILL BRISCOE

A TIP FOR TODAY

God has a plan for your life, a divine calling. How you respond to it will determine the direction you take and the contributions you make.

Faith looks back and draws courage; hope looks ahead and keeps desire alive.

JOHN ELDREDGE

Love is the seed of all hope. It is the enticement to trust, to risk, to try, and to go on.

GLORIA GAITHER

A PRAYER FOR TODAY

Dear Lord, let my hopes begin and end with You. When I am discouraged, let me turn to You. When I am weak, let me find strength in You. You are my Father, and I will place my faith, my trust, and my hopes in You, this day and forever. Amen

TODAY'S THOUGHTS

My thoughts about the power of hope and the rewards of trusting God.

_____

_____

_____

_____

_____

_____

_____

_____

_____

DAY 26

YOUR VERY BRIGHT FUTURE

For I know the thoughts that I think toward you,
says the Lord, thoughts of peace and not of evil, to
give you a future and a hope.
Then you will call upon Me and go and pray to Me,
and I will listen to you.

—

JEREMIAH 29:11-12 NKJV

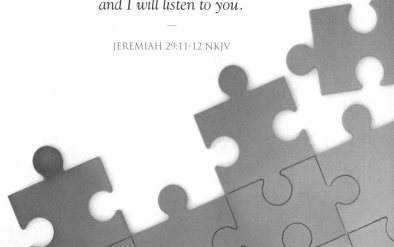

Our future may look fearfully intimidating,
yet we can look up to the Engineer of the Universe,
confident that nothing escapes His attention or
slips out of the control of those strong hands.

—

ELISABETH ELLIOT

Because we are saved by a risen Christ, we can have hope for the future, no matter how troublesome our present circumstances may seem. After all, God has promised that we are His throughout eternity. And, He has told us that we must place our hopes in Him.

Of course, we will face disappointments and failures while we are here on earth, but these are only temporary defeats. This world can be a place of trials and tribulations, but when we place our trust in the Giver of all things good, we are secure. God has promised us peace, joy, and eternal life. And God keeps His promises today, tomorrow, and forever.

Are you willing to place your future in the hands of a loving and all-knowing God? Do you trust in the ultimate goodness of His plan for your life? Will you face today's challenges with optimism and hope? You should. After all, God created you for a very important purpose: His purpose. And you still have important work to do: His work.

Today, as you live in the present and look to the future, remember that God has a plan for you. Act—and believe—accordingly.

LET GOD BE YOUR GUIDE

The Bible promises that God will guide you if you let Him. Your job, of course, is to let Him. But sometimes, you will be tempted to do otherwise. Sometimes, you'll be tempted to go along with the crowd; other times, you'll be tempted to do things your way, not God's way. When you feel those temptations, you must resist them, or else.

What will you allow to guide you through the coming day: your own desires (or, for that matter, the desires of your peers)? Or will you allow God to lead the way? The answer should be obvious. You should let God be your guide. When you entrust your life to Him completely and without reservation, God will give you the strength to meet any challenge, the courage to face any trial, and the wisdom to live in His righteousness. So trust Him today and seek His guidance. When you do, your character will most certainly take care of itself, and your next step will most assuredly be the right one.

MORE FROM GOD'S WORD ABOUT
HIS GUIDANCE

In all your ways acknowledge Him, and He shall direct your paths.

PROVERBS 3:6 NKJV

For now we see indistinctly, as in a mirror, but then face to face. Now I know in part, but then I will know fully, as I am fully known.

1 CORINTHIANS 13:12 HCSB

However, each one must live his life in the situation the Lord assigned when God called him.

1 CORINTHIANS 7:17 HCSB

The earth and everything in it, the world and its inhabitants, belong to the Lord.

PSALM 24:1 HCSB

My cup runs over. Surely goodness and mercy shall follow me all the days of my life; and I will dwell in the house of the Lord forever.

PSALM 23:5-6 NKJV

MORE POWERFUL IDEAS ABOUT YOUR FUTURE

The future lies all before us. Shall it only be a slight advance upon what we usually do? Ought it not to be a bound, a leap forward to altitudes of endeavor and success undreamed of before?

ANNIE ARMSTRONG

Every experience God gives us, every person he brings into our lives, is the perfect preparation for the future that only he can see.

CORRIE TEN BOOM

The Christian believes in a fabulous future.

BILLY GRAHAM

A TIP FOR TODAY

God will guide you if you let Him. Your job is to acknowledge Him and to follow closely in the footsteps of His Son.

Fix your eyes upon the Lord! Do it once. Do it daily. Do it constantly. Look at the Lord and keep looking at Him.

CHARLES SWINDOLL

A PRAYER FOR TODAY

Dear Lord, as I look to the future, I will place my trust in You. If I become discouraged, I will turn to You. If I am afraid, I will seek strength in You. You are my Father, and I will place my hope, my trust, and my faith in You. Amen

TODAY'S THOUGHTS

My thoughts about the bright future—and the eternal life—that is mine through Christ.

_____

_____

_____

_____

_____

_____

_____

_____

_____

_____

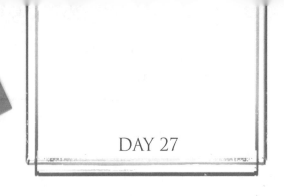

DAY 27

THE VALUE SYSTEM YOU CAN DEPEND ON

*Do what is right and good in the Lord's sight, so that
you may prosper and so that you may enter and
possess the good land the Lord your God
swore to give your fathers.*

—

DEUTERONOMY 6:18 HCSB

If you want to be proactive in the way you live your life,
if you want to influence your life's direction, if you want
your life to exhibit the qualities you find desirable,
and if you want to live with integrity, then you need to
know what your values are, decide to embrace them,
and practice them every day.

—

JOHN MAXWELL

Whether you realize it or not, your character is shaped by your values. From the time your alarm clock wakes you in the morning until the moment you lay your head on the pillow at night, your actions are guided by the values that you hold most dear. If you're a thoughtful believer, then those values are shaped by the Word of God.

Society seeks to impose its set of values upon you, however these values are often contrary to God's Word (and thus contrary to your own best interests). The world makes promises that it simply cannot fulfill. It promises happiness, contentment, prosperity, and abundance. But genuine abundance is not a by-product of possessions or status; it is a by-product of your thoughts, your actions, and your relationship with God. The world's promises are incomplete and deceptive; God's promises are unfailing. Your challenge, then, is to build your value system upon the firm foundation of God's promises . . . nothing else will suffice.

As a citizen of the 21st century, you live in a fast-changing world that is filled with countless opportunities to make big-time mistakes. The world seems to cry, "Worship me with your time, your money, your energy, and your thoughts!" But God commands otherwise: He commands you to worship Him and Him alone; everything else must be secondary.

Do you want to strengthen your character? If so, then you must build your life upon a value system that puts God first. So, when you're faced with a difficult choice or a powerful temptation, seek God's counsel and trust the counsel that He gives. Invite God into your heart and live according to His commandments. Study His Word and talk to Him often. When you do, you will share in the abundance and peace that only God can give.

IN DIFFICULT TIMES, GOD TEACHES AND LEADS

Complete spiritual maturity is never achieved in a day, or in a year, or even in a lifetime. The journey toward spiritual maturity is an ongoing process that continues, day by day, throughout every stage of life. Every stage of life has its opportunities and its challenges, and if we're wise, we continue to seek God's guidance as each new chapter of life unfolds.

From time to time, all of us encounter circumstances that test our faith. When we encounter life's inevitable tragedies, trials, uncertainties, and disappointments, we may be tempted to blame God or to rebel against Him. But the Bible reminds us that the trials of life should be viewed as opportunities for growth: "Consider it a great joy, my brothers, whenever you experience various trials, knowing that the testing of your faith produces endurance. But endurance must do its complete work, so that you may be mature and complete, lacking nothing" (James 1:2-4 HCSB).

Have you recently encountered one of life's inevitable tests? If so, remember that God still has lessons that He intends to teach you. So ask yourself this: What lesson is God trying to teach me today?

You will get untold flak for prioritizing God's revealed and present will for your life over man's . . .
but, boy, is it worth it.

———

BETH MOORE

MORE FROM GOD'S WORD ABOUT VALUES

You will know the truth, and the truth will set you free.

JOHN 8:32 HCSB

God's Way is not a matter of mere talk; it's an empowered life.

1 CORINTHIANS 4:20 MSG

Walk in a manner worthy of the God who calls you into His own kingdom and glory.

1 THESSALONIANS 2:12 NASB

Therefore, since we have this ministry, as we have received mercy, we do not give up. Instead, we have renounced shameful secret things, not walking in deceit or distorting God's message, but in God's sight we commend ourselves to every person's conscience by an open display of the truth.

2 CORINTHIANS 4:1-2 HCSB

We must not become tired of doing good. We will receive our harvest of eternal life at the right time if we do not give up.

GALATIANS 6:9 NCV

MORE POWERFUL IDEAS ABOUT OBEDIENCE

Obedience is the outward expression of your love of God.

HENRY BLACKABY

God's love for His children is unconditional, no strings attached. But, God's blessings on our lives do come with a condition—obedience. If we are to receive the fullness of God's blessings, we must obey Him and keep His commandments.

JIM GALLERY

We cannot rely on God's promises without obeying his commandments.

JOHN CALVIN

Trials and sufferings teach us to obey the Lord by faith, and we soon learn that obedience pays off in joyful ways.

BILL BRIGHT

A TIP FOR TODAY

When you place your faith in God, life becomes a grand adventure energized by the power of God.

A PRAYER FOR TODAY

Lord, help me value the things in this world that are really valuable: my life, my family, and my relationship with You. Amen

TODAY'S THOUGHTS

My thoughts about the rewards of obeying God.

_____

_____

_____

_____

_____

_____

_____

_____

_____

_____

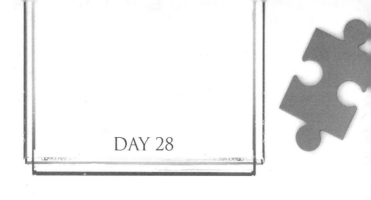

DAY 28

THE ULTIMATE PROTECTION

The Lord is my rock, my fortress, and my deliverer.
—

PSALM 18:2 HCSB

Being loved by Him whose opinion matters most
gives us the security to risk loving, too—
even loving ourselves.

—

GLORIA GAITHER

The hand of God encircles us and comforts us in times of adversity. In times of hardship, He restores our strength; in times of sorrow, He dries our tears. When we are troubled, or weak, or embittered, God is as near as our next breath.

God has promised to protect us, and He intends to fulfill His promise. In a world filled with dangers and temptations, God is the ultimate armor. In a world filled with misleading messages, God's Word is the ultimate truth. In a world filled with more frustrations than we can count, God's Son offers the ultimate peace.

Will you accept God's peace and wear God's armor against the dangers of our world? Hopefully so, because when you do, you can live courageously, knowing that you possess the ultimate protection: God's unfailing love for you.

YOU ARE PROTECTED

Although God has probably guided you through many struggles and more than a few difficult days, you may still find your faith stretched to the limit whenever you encounter adversity, uncertainty, or unwelcome changes. But the good news is this: even though your circumstances may change, God's love for you does not.

The next time you find yourself facing a fear-provoking situation, remember that no challenge is too big for your Heavenly Father, not even yours. And while you're thinking about the scope of God's power and His love, ask yourself which is stronger: your faith or your fear. The answer should be obvious.

Wherever you are, God is there, too. And, because He cares for you today and always, you are protected.

Under heaven's lock and key, we are protected
by the most efficient security system available:
the power of God.

—

CHARLES SWINDOLL

MORE FROM GOD'S WORD ABOUT
HIS PROTECTION

The Lord bless you and protect you; the Lord make His face shine on you, and be gracious to you.

NUMBERS 6:24-25 HCSB

The Lord your God in your midst, The Mighty One, will save; He will rejoice over you with gladness, He will quiet you with His love, He will rejoice over you with singing.

ZEPHANIAH 3:17 NKJV

God is my shield, saving those whose hearts are true and right.

PSALM 7:10 NLT

Those who trust the Lord are like Mount Zion, which sits unmoved forever. As the mountains surround Jerusalem, the Lord surrounds his people now and forever.

PSALM 125:1-2 NCV

Finally, my brethren, be strong in the Lord and in the power of His might. Put on the whole armor of God, that you may be able to stand against the wiles of the devil.

EPHESIANS 6:10-11 NKJV

MORE POWERFUL IDEAS ABOUT GOD'S PROTECTION

The Rock of Ages is the great sheltering encirclement.

OSWALD CHAMBERS

In all the old castles of England, there was a place called the keep. It was always the strongest and best protected place in the castle, and in it were hidden all who were weak and helpless and unable to defend themselves in times of danger. Shall we be afraid to hide ourselves in the keeping power of our Divine Keeper, who neither slumbers nor sleeps, and who has promised to preserve our going out and our coming in, from this time forth and even forever more?

HANNAH WHITALL SMITH

The promises of God's Word sustain us in our suffering, and we know Jesus sympathizes and empathizes with us in our darkest hour.

BILL BRIGHT

A TIP FOR TODAY

When you invite the love of God into your heart, everything changes . . . including you.

A PRAYER FOR TODAY

Dear Heavenly Father, You have blessed us with a love that is infinite and eternal. We will be Your loving servants, Father, today and throughout eternity. And, we will show our love for You by sharing Your message and Your love with a world that desperately needs the healing touch of the Master's hand. Amen

TODAY'S THOUGHTS

My thoughts about God's love and His promise of protection.

_____

_____

_____

_____

_____

_____

_____

_____

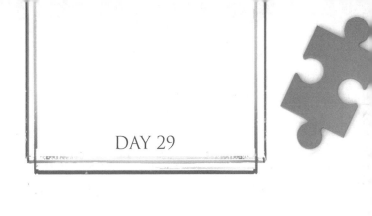

DAY 29

MAKING PEACE
WITH YOUR PAST

Do not remember the past events, pay no attention
to things of old. Look, I am about to do something
new; even now it is coming. Do you not see it?
Indeed, I will make a way in the wilderness,
rivers in the desert.

—

ISAIAH 43:18-19 HCSB

The pages of your past cannot be rewritten,
but the pages of your tomorrows are blank.

—

ZIG ZIGLAR

The American theologian Reinhold Niebuhr composed a profoundly simple verse that came to be known as the Serenity Prayer: "God, grant me the serenity to accept the things I cannot change, the courage to change the things I can, and the wisdom to know the difference." Niebuhr's words are far easier to recite than they are to live by. Why? Because most of us want life to unfold in accordance with our own wishes and timetables. But sometimes God has other plans.

One of the things that fits nicely into the category of "things we cannot change" is the past. Yet even though we know that the past is unchangeable, many of us continue to invest energy worrying about the unfairness of yesterday (when we should, instead, be focusing on the opportunities of today and the promises of tomorrow). Author Hannah Whitall Smith observed, "How changed our lives would be if we could only fly through the days on wings of surrender and trust!" These words remind us that even when we cannot understand the past, we must trust God and accept His will.

So, if you've endured a difficult past, accept it and learn from it, but don't spend too much time here in the precious present fretting over memories of the unchangeable past. Instead, trust God's plan and look to the future. After all, the future is where everything that's going to happen to you from this moment on is going to take place.

ACCEPTING THE PAST, LIVING IN THE PRESENT

Man made plans are fallible; God's plans are not. Yet whenever life takes an unexpected turn, we are tempted to fall into the spiritual traps of worry, self-pity, or bitterness. God intends that we do otherwise.

The old saying is familiar: "Forgive and forget." But when we have been hurt badly, forgiveness is often difficult and forgetting is downright impossible. Since we can't forget yesterday's troubles, we should learn from them. Yesterday has much to teach us about tomorrow. We may learn from the past, but we should never live in the past. God has given each of us a glorious day: this one. And it's up to each of us to use this day as faithful stewards, not as embittered historians.

So if you're trying to forget the past, don't waste your time. Instead, try a different approach: learn to accept

the past and live in the present. Then, you can focus your thoughts and your energies, not on the struggles of yesterday, but instead on the profound opportunities that God has placed before you today.

Leave the broken, irreversible past in God's hands,
and step out into the invincible future with Him.

—

OSWALD CHAMBERS

MORE FROM GOD'S WORD ABOUT
ACCEPTING THE PAST

All bitterness, anger and wrath, insult and slander must be removed from you, along with all wickedness. And be kind and compassionate to one another, forgiving one another, just as God also forgave you in Christ.

EPHESIANS 4:31-32 HCSB

I have learned, in whatsoever state I am, therewith to be content.

PHILIPPIANS 4:11 KJV

Brothers, I do not consider myself to have taken hold of it. But one thing I do: forgetting what is behind and reaching forward to what is ahead, I pursue as my goal the prize promised by God's heavenly call in Christ Jesus.

PHILIPPIANS 3:13-14 HCSB

For if you forgive people their wrongdoing, your heavenly Father will forgive you as well. But if you don't forgive people, your Father will not forgive your wrongdoing.

MATTHEW 6:14-15 HCSB

185

MORE POWERFUL IDEAS ABOUT
ACCEPTING THE PAST

Our yesterdays teach us how to savor our todays and tomorrows.

PATSY CLAIRMONT

The devil keeps so many of us stuck in our weakness. He reminds us of our pasts when we ought to remind him of his future—he doesn't have one.

FRANKLIN GRAHAM

If you are God's child, you are no longer bound to your past or to what you were. You are a brand new creature in Christ Jesus.

KAY ARTHUR

A TIP FOR TODAY

The past is past, so don't invest all your energy there. If you're focused on the past, change your focus. If you're living in the past, move on.

We need to be at peace with our past, content with our present, and sure about our future, knowing they are all in God's hands.

JOYCE MEYER

186

A PRAYER FOR TODAY

Heavenly Father, free me from anger, resentment, and envy. When I am bitter, I cannot feel the peace that You intend for my life. Keep me mindful that forgiveness is Your commandment, and help me accept the past, treasure the present, and trust the future . . . to You. Amen

TODAY'S THOUGHTS

My thoughts about the rewards of focusing on the present, not the past.

_____

_____

_____

_____

_____

_____

_____

_____

DAY 30

FOLLOW HIM

Then Jesus said to His disciples,
"If anyone wants to come with Me, he must
deny himself, take up his cross, and follow Me.
For whoever wants to save his life will lose it, but
whoever loses his life because of Me will find it."

—

MATTHEW 16:24-25 HCSB

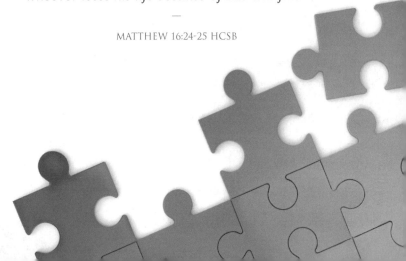

You who suffer take heart.
Christ is the answer to sorrow.

———

BILLY GRAHAM

Jesus walks with you. Are you walking with Him seven days a week, and not just on Sunday mornings? Are you a seven-day-a-week Christian who carries your faith with you to work each day, or do you try to keep Jesus at a "safe" distance when you're not sitting in church? Hopefully, you understand the wisdom of walking with Christ all day every day.

Jesus loved you so much that He endured unspeakable humiliation and suffering for you. How will you respond to Christ's sacrifice? Will you take up His cross and follow Him—during good times and tough times—or will you choose another path? When you place your hopes squarely at the foot of the cross, when you place Jesus squarely at the center of your life, you will be blessed.

Do you seek to fulfill God's purpose for your life? Do you seek spiritual abundance? Would you like to partake in "the peace that passes all understanding"? Then follow Christ. Follow Him by picking up His cross today and every day that you live. When you do, you will quickly discover that Christ's love has the power to change everything, including you.

YOUR ETERNAL JOURNEY

Eternal life is not an event that begins when you die. Eternal life begins when you invite Jesus into your heart right here on earth. So it's important to remember that God's plans for you are not limited to the ups and downs of everyday life. If you've allowed Jesus to reign over your heart, you've already begun your eternal journey.

Today, give praise to the Creator for His priceless gift, the gift of eternal life. And then, when you've offered Him your thanks and your praise, share His Good News with all who cross your path.

In the midst of the pressure and the heat,
I am confident His hand is on my life, developing
my faith until I display His glory, transforming me
into a vessel of honor that pleases Him!

—

ANNE GRAHAM LOTZ

MORE FROM GOD'S WORD ABOUT
FOLLOWING CHRIST

*Then he told them what they could expect for themselves:
"Anyone who intends to come with me has to let me lead."*

LUKE 9:23 MSG

I've laid down a pattern for you. What I've done, you do.

JOHN 13:15 MSG

*No one can serve two masters. Either he will hate the one and
love the other, or he will be devoted to the one and despise the
other.*

MATTHEW 6:24 NIV

*Whoever is not willing to carry the cross and follow me is not
worthy of me. Those who try to hold on to their lives will give
up true life. Those who give up their lives for me will hold on
to true life.*

MATTHEW 10:38-39 NCV

*If anyone would come after me, he must deny himself and take
up his cross and follow me.*

MARK 8:34 NIV

MORE POWERFUL IDEAS ABOUT
FOLLOWING CHRIST

Jesus Christ is not a security from storms. He is perfect security in storms.

KATHY TROCCOLI

Sometimes we get tired of the burdens of life, but we know that Jesus Christ will meet us at the end of life's journey. And, that makes all the difference.

BILLY GRAHAM

The Lord gets His best soldiers out of the highlands of affliction.

C. H. SPURGEON

A TIP FOR TODAY

If you want to be a little more like Jesus, learn about His teachings, follow in His footsteps, and obey His commandments.

God takes us through struggles and difficulties so that we might become increasingly committed to Him.

CHARLES SWINDOLL

A PRAYER FOR TODAY

Dear Jesus, because I am Your disciple, I will trust You, I will obey Your teachings, and I will share Your Good News. You have given me life abundant and life eternal, and I will follow You today and forever. Amen

TODAY'S THOUGHTS

My thoughts about the genuine joys and eternal rewards of following Jesus.

_____

_____

_____

_____

_____

_____

_____

_____

_____

_____

We can all humbly say in
the sincerity of faith,
"I am loved; I am called;
I am secure."

—

FRANKLIN GRAHAM

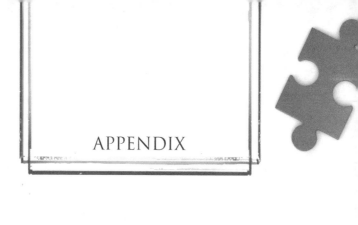

APPENDIX

MORE FROM
GOD'S WORD

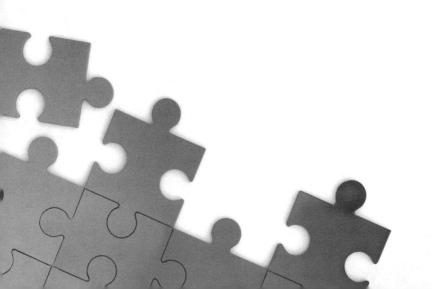

ABUNDANCE

I have come that they may have life, and that they may have it more abundantly.

JOHN 10:10 NKJV

And God is able to make every grace overflow to you, so that in every way, always having everything you need, you may excel in every good work.

2 CORINTHIANS 9:8 HCSB

Until now you have asked for nothing in My name. Ask and you will receive, that your joy may be complete.

JOHN 16:24 HCSB

*Come to terms with God and be at peace;
in this way good will come to you.*

JOB 22:21 HCSB

My cup runs over. Surely goodness and mercy shall follow me all the days of my life; and I will dwell in the house of the Lord forever.

PSALM 23:5-6 NKJV

DREAMS

Now may the God of hope fill you with all joy and peace in believing, so that you may overflow with hope by the power of the Holy Spirit.

ROMANS 15:13 HCSB

Where there is no vision, the people perish. . . .

PROVERBS 29:18 KJV

Be of good courage, and he shall strengthen your heart, all ye that hope in the LORD.

PSALM 31:24 KJV

Therefore, as we have opportunity, we must work for the good of all, especially for those who belong to the household of faith.

GALATIANS 6:10 HCSB

But as it is written: What no eye has seen and no ear has heard, and what has never come into a man's heart, is what God has prepared for those who love Him.

1 CORINTHIANS 2:9 HCSB

197

DISCIPLESHIP

Anyone who listens to me is happy, watching at my doors every day, waiting by the posts of my doorway. For the one who finds me finds life and obtains favor from the Lord, but the one who sins against me harms himself; all who hate me love death.

PROVERBS 8:34-36 HCSB

He has told you men what is good and what it is the Lord requires of you: Only to act justly, to love faithfulness, and to walk humbly with your God.

MICAH 6:8 HCSB

Therefore, be imitators of God, as dearly loved children.

EPHESIANS 5:1 HCSB

We always pray for you that our God will consider you worthy of His calling, and will, by His power, fulfill every desire for goodness and the work of faith, so that the name of our Lord Jesus will be glorified by you, and you by Him, according to the grace of our God and the Lord Jesus Christ.

2 THESSALONIANS 1:11-12 HCSB

SILENCE

Happy is the man who finds wisdom, and the man who gains understanding.

PROVERBS 3:13 NKJV

*I sought the Lord, and He heard me,
and delivered me from all my fears.*

PSALM 34:4 NKJV

Be still, and know that I am God.

PSALM 46:10 NKJV

Be silent before the Lord and wait expectantly for Him.

PSALM 37:7 HCSB

In quietness and confidence shall be your strength.

ISAIAH 30:15 NKJV

I am not alone, because the Father is with Me.

JOHN 16:32 HCSB

MATURITY

A wise man will hear, and will increase learning;
and a man of understanding shall attain
unto wise counsels. . . .

PROVERBS 1:5 KJV

Do not be conformed to this age, but be transformed by the
renewing of your mind, so that you may discern what is the
good, pleasing, and perfect will of God.

ROMANS 12:2 HCSB

When I was a child, I spoke like a child, I thought like a child,
I reasoned like a child. When I became a man, I put aside
childish things.

1 CORINTHIANS 13:11 HCSB

Consider it a great joy, my brothers, whenever you experience
various trials, knowing that the testing of your faith produces
endurance. But endurance must do its complete work, so that
you may be mature and complete, lacking nothing.

JAMES 1:2-4 HCSB

EXAMPLE

Love and truth form a good leader; sound leadership is founded on loving integrity.

PROVERBS 20:28 MSG

You should be an example to the believers in speech, in conduct, in love, in faith, in purity.

1 TIMOTHY 4:12 HCSB

Therefore since we also have such a large cloud of witnesses surrounding us, let us lay aside every weight and the sin that so easily ensnares us, and run with endurance the race that lies before us.

HEBREWS 12:1 HCSB

Set an example of good works yourself, with integrity and dignity in your teaching.

TITUS 2:7 HCSB

Do everything without grumbling and arguing, so that you may be blameless and pure.

PHILIPPIANS 2:14-15 HCSB

ANGER

Everyone must be quick to hear, slow to speak, and slow to anger, for man's anger does not accomplish God's righteousness.

JAMES 1:19-20 HCSB

A patient person [shows] great understanding, but a quick-tempered one promotes foolishness.

PROVERBS 14:29 HCSB

But now you must also put away all the following: anger, wrath, malice, slander, and filthy language from your mouth.

COLOSSIANS 3:8 HCSB

Don't let your spirit rush to be angry, for anger abides in the heart of fools.

ECCLESIASTES 7:9 HCSB

All bitterness, anger and wrath, insult and slander must be removed from you, along with all wickedness. And be kind and compassionate to one another, forgiving one another, just as God also forgave you in Christ.

EPHESIANS 4:31-32 HCSB

GENEROSITY

The generous soul will be made rich, and he who waters will also be watered himself.

PROVERBS 11:25 NKJV

Freely you have received, freely give.

MATTHEW 10:8 NKJV

As each one has received a gift, minister it to one another, as good stewards of the manifold grace of God.

1 PETER 4:10 NKJV

But this I say: He who sows sparingly will also reap sparingly, and he who sows bountifully will also reap bountifully. So let each one give as he purposes in his heart, not grudgingly or of necessity; for God loves a cheerful giver.

2 CORINTHIANS 9:6-7 NKJV

Cast your bread upon the waters, for you will find it after many days.

ECCLESIASTES 11:1 NKJV

GOD'S TIMING

*Wait for the Lord; be courageous and
let your heart be strong. Wait for the Lord.*

PSALM 27:14 HCSB

*He said to them, "It is not for you to know times or periods that
the Father has set by His own authority."*

ACTS 1:7 HCSB

*He has made everything appropriate in its time. He has also put
eternity in their hearts, but man cannot discover the work God
has done from beginning to end.*

ECCLESIASTES 3:11 HCSB

*Therefore the Lord is waiting to show you mercy, and is rising
up to show you compassion, for the Lord is a just God. Happy
are all who wait patiently for Him.*

ISAIAH 30:18 HCSB

*For My thoughts are not your thoughts, and your ways are not
My ways. For as heaven is higher than earth, so My ways are
higher than your ways, and My thoughts than your thoughts.*

ISAIAH 55:8-9 HCSB

LOVE

As in water face reflects face, so a man's heart reveals the man.

PROVERBS 27:19 NKJV

No one has greater love than this, that someone would lay down his life for his friends.

JOHN 15:13 HCSB

Though I speak with the tongues of men and of angels, but have not love, I have become sounding brass or a clanging cymbal.

1 CORINTHIANS 13:1 NKJV

Dear friends, if God loved us in this way, we also must love one another.

1 JOHN 4:11 HCSB

Above all, keep your love for one another at full strength, since love covers a multitude of sins.

1 PETER 4:8 HCSB

ENCOURAGING OTHERS

*I want their hearts to be encouraged and joined together in love,
so that they may have all the riches of assured understanding,
and have the knowledge of God's mystery—Christ.*

COLOSSIANS 2:2 HCSB

*And let us be concerned about one another
in order to promote love and good works.*

HEBREWS 10:24 HCSB

*Carry one another's burdens; in this way you will fulfill the law
of Christ.*

GALATIANS 6:2 HCSB

*But encourage each other daily, while it is still called today, so
that none of you is hardened by sin's deception.*

HEBREWS 3:13 HCSB

*Anxiety in a man's heart weighs it down, but a good word
cheers it up.*

PROVERBS 12:25 HCSB

LEADERSHIP

For an overseer, as God's manager, must be blameless, not arrogant, not quick tempered, not addicted to wine, not a bully, not greedy for money.

TITUS 1:7 HCSB

According to the grace given to us, we have different gifts: If prophecy, use it according to the standard of faith; if service, in service; if teaching, in teaching; if exhorting, in exhortation; giving, with generosity; leading, with diligence; showing mercy, with cheerfulness.

ROMANS 12:6-8 HCSB

Shepherd God's flock among you, not overseeing out of compulsion but freely, according to God's will; not for the money but eagerly.

1 PETER 5:2 HCSB

And we exhort you, brothers: warn those who are lazy, comfort the discouraged, help the weak, be patient with everyone.

1 THESSALONIANS 5:14 HCSB

207

And if you believe,
you will receive whatever you ask for
in prayer.

—

MATTHEW 21:22 HCSB

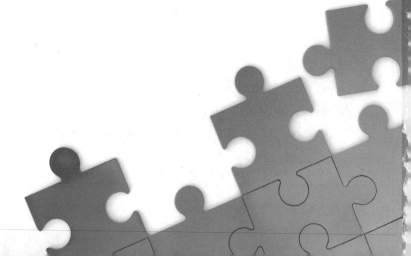